THE MAKING OF THE NATION

William Kilbourn

THE
MAKING
OF
THE
NATION

A Century of Challenge

THE CANADIAN CENTENNIAL LIBRARY

Text for picture albums by Pierre Berton and Ken Lefolii

THE CANADIAN CENTENNIAL LIBRARY

WEEKEND MAGAZINE/MCCLELLAND AND STEWART LIMITED

Pierre Berton, *Editor-in-chief;* Frank Newfeld, *Art Director;* Ken Lefolii, *Managing Editor*

THE CANADIAN CENTENNIAL PUBLISHING CO., LTD.

150 SIMCOE STREET, TORONTO, CANADA

CONTENTS

PROLOGUE:

WHO AND WHAT WE ARE

Once upon a time, many worlds ago, before there was a Germany or half the earth's nations were thought of, when medieval emperors ruled Middle Europe and all the Russias and a Napoleon governed France, when the pound sterling commanded the commerce of the seven seas and the Pax Britannica protected it, when the factories of Lancashire and the blackening Midlands were leading mankind past the threshold of the industrial age and the young republic that called itself the last best hope of earth had just freed its slaves and fought the first total war in history, in a time before the lesser breeds of Asia had quite become the white man's burden or the white man theirs, and before Livingstone, vanished in the darkness of Africa, had been found by the first ambassador from the new mass media, Stanley of the New York *Herald* – long ago in that far distant age, on the first day of July, 1867, the Dominion of Canada was born.

The new country consisted of a three-thousand-mile scattering of outposts and settlements and sub-arctic wilderness. It was the handiwork of an inspired little group of colonial politicians who seized upon it as the solution to a crisis in their affairs, and used every skill of bargaining and blarney, private intrigue and public campaign, to complete the job. By 1871, when it took final shape (barring a couple of island provinces that came in later), Canada was the second largest country on the face of the globe, thirty times the size of the parent whose blessing and protection had made it possible.

Except for Canadians themselves, however, and a few Britishers like the colonial secretary, Lord Carnarvon, nobody took it very seriously. The House of Commons at Westminster was three-quarters empty when it passed the British North America Act, though it filled up immediately afterwards for the debate on a dog tax bill. Oh, the English knew what they were

doing, all right – their fits of absent-mindedness were for acquiring empires, not for sloughing them off. It was just that the idea of Canada bored them, as it has bored most Englishmen ever since. That same year the Russian czar made a white elephant sale of Alaska to Mr. Secretary Seward of the United States – the only large piece of the continent's northern mainland that was not to be Canada's. The price was $7,200,000 – two cents an acre – and a lot of angry Americans thought their man had been soft-sawdered.

"Power," said Napoleon, "is never ridiculous." Canada was not powerful. This preposterous, monstrous accident of a place – what images would conjure its enormity? What in heaven's name, if one were an 1867 Adam, new-naming things in the Garden, what would one call it? A whale-sized dormouse, asleep in the forest, nibbling a prairie or a piece of tundra? A giant clam, silent and foetal in the earth's oldest shell? A nine-thousand-room hotel with the lower floors half occupied, the structural beams still showing far above, a bit of camping on the upper girders, and a huge annex still on the drafting boards? Kingdom is the name the Fathers of Confederation wanted to give it but the British were afraid the word might just set off another war with the United States. So they settled for Dominion, which was Biblical, sonorous and vague.

The nineteenth century knew two kinds of nation. One, like the nations of Europe, had a past and had grown imperceptibly by custom and habit out of some prehistoric gathering of clans, even if the final act, like Italy's, was deliberate. The other kind of nation, without a past, was created in a single stroke of revolutionary violence by an act of the rational will, like the American republics of the New World. Canada was clearly neither of these. By most definitions of the word, it was not a nation at all. A century afterwards, it is still extant, still not fossilized or dissolved into

6

its original parts or swallowed up by a hungry neighbour. It has grown prodigiously, albeit by primitive booms and crashes, manic leaps from euphoria to despair and back again, and it has acquired a kind of coherence and maturity. Yet as it enters its second century it has not quite become a nation. It is not even a nationette, as that disgusted prisoner of World War II Toronto, the English artist Wyndham Lewis, called it – although there are plenty of native identity-mongers and boosters of Cancult who have done their best to make it one. Until 1965, a Canadian schoolchild could claim with some pride that his was unique among the world's peoples in not having a flag: he could choose his own – UN, Union Jack, fleur-de-lis or Elmer the Safety Elephant – as the spirit moved him. The situation had its advantages. An American, Mort Sahl, on being asked by one of Canada's angry old radio-personality patriots what he thought of a country that did not have a national flag, replied, "Well, it's a start."

Canada at the ripe age of one hundred years was something a little less a nation, and in some ways just possibly preferable. It has been for most of its history a good provincial sort of place, one of Western civilization's most reliable experimental farms, a place where a person had time to grow and was free to make mistakes. But until the second half of the twentieth century, as sure as Dick Whittington had to go to London, the most gifted Canadians, if they were to fulfil what they had in them, often as not had to leave for one of the world capitals. It is symptomatic that the greatest of our countrymen and perhaps the only one yet marked for immortality in the annals of mankind, William Osler, should have gone to the United States to make his crucial contribution to the practice of medicine, and to Oxford to crown his career. One of the ultimate tests of nationhood is the condition of the arts, for they need a local habitation and a name

just as much as they need to transcend national boundaries. Specifically, one must ask whether a country's artists have a real choice, in order to follow their vocation, between staying home and leaving. Towards the end of Canada's first hundred years there were clear signs at last of the arts emerging from their provincial condition, but the change had been long in coming, and many of the best artists, especially in new forms like film and television, were still departing for London and Paris and New York.

There were signs too that in the realm of power, Canada might assume the last crowning attributes of political independence, the symbols and the realities out of which the psychology of nationhood can grow. These too had been slow in coming. It took forty years to establish a token foreign office and yet another generation for Canada to begin to have an independent foreign policy. It took nearly ninety years for Canadians to prefer the final judgments of their own supreme court to those of a committee of British privy-councillors. It took eighty years to establish Canadian citizenship, ninety-eight years for a national flag to be flown, and even longer for Canadians to assume the power to change their constitution. It took seventy years to renounce the receipt of hereditary titles and other faintly ludicrous scrapings from the lower registers of the honours list of a society whose class divisions and accents had little to do with the realities of Canadian life. It took seventy-five years to acquire the beginnings of a Canadian honours list with the establishment of the Canada Medal, and another quarter century to begin looking for the first recipient. It was seventy-two years before the Canadian head of state set foot on Canadian soil, and subsequent visits have been rare and brief. Other countries, such as the United Kingdom, appeared to find it useful and necessary to have native, resident heads of state. Canada was moving into her second century without one.

Canadians have been accustomed to define themselves by saying what they are not. Long before 1867 they were adepts in the art of saying No. Four times they had actually beaten off attempts on their independence by foreign invaders – in the two wars of 1776 and 1812 and in the little unofficial invasions of 1838-39 and 1866. The French Canadians said No very effectively to the British conquest, and to all the attempts to assimilate or submerge them since. They said No to the French Revolution and all it stood for, at least until it could be considered to have blown itself out and become politically safe, sometime about 1960. They also said No to the American Revolution, as did the settlers who left their homes in the Thirteen Colonies and came here to settle in the wilderness. Canadians said No consistently to the Mother Country on the questions of imperial federation, imperial armies and navies, and common foreign policy. While one Canadian political party could win popular support by identifying itself with the practice of saying No to the British, the other won elections by saying No to the Americans.

The earlier acts of no-saying, before 1867, showed courage and a certain grim, stubborn kind of uncommon sense. But those in the twentieth century, often as not, displayed an unlovely adolescent petulance. The historian Frank Underhill declared that his fellow Canadians must have been born saying no; they were eighteen million Peter Pans who would not grow up, and if they persisted in indulging themselves much longer they would certainly end up as nothing better than the Ulster of North America.

But to look on the cheerier side, at least there can be no such thing as an Un-Canadian Activities Committee – we are not much given to the double negative, even if anyone could manage to define what the Un-Canadian activity was. The heartiest maple-leafer is unlikely to risk being so ridiculous as to come right out for a Canadian counterpart of the process known as Americanization or the public festival officially designated as I Am An American Day. We are more apt to scrap the BNA Act, quietly and in little bits, than to seal it in helium under glass and display it as a relic cure for a deficiency of red-bloodedness.

Even the very name Canada is open to the power of negative thinking. An eminent Canadian sociologist, a native of Austria, has pointed out that where he came from the word is pronounced *keine dah* and means "nobody there." The name Canada is supposed

Marking Canada-U.S. border, 1876. "This is Nowheresville. But if you are nothing, you may be anything."

to derive from what the Indians kept yelling at our discoverer, Jacques Cartier, as they pointed up river, so that for what it is worth *"Kanata! Kanata!"* means "Yonder are our wigwams!" There was another view which held that the Indians must already have conversed with Portuguese fishermen drying the cod they had taken off the Grand Banks and who, unlike Cartier, did not realize they had discovered Canada. This view suggested that the Indians were really saying *"Aca nada"* in Portuguese, so that Canada means, "There's nothing here." No matter that the story is discredited ("Wigwams," or "Village," is what we are, whether we like it or not), its intention points to the heart of things. This is a nothing place. Nowheresville. And here is the trick of it. If you are nothing you may also be anything. You may be a map or a model of everything. You might even hope someday to become something – "a something possible, a chance," as a novelist once called Canada. The scholar and former diplomat Douglas LePan has found the

8

Canadian passport a useful image for all this. The little blue booklet stamped in gold is one of the world's more precious commodities, the one most often used by those operating international rackets or spy systems. Its popularity lies not just in the fact one can travel almost anywhere with it, but that one can speak almost any language with almost any accent, be a member of almost any race, "English or French or Ukrainian or Polish or Chinese, and still be a Canadian. One can, in fact, be almost anyone and still be a Canadian. To be a Canadian is to have a passport to the whole world."

The Canadian is possibly closer to the role of the later twentieth century hero, or anti-hero, than anyone else. A European or an Asian, whether he likes it or not, is clothed in habits of body and soul bred by millenia of cultural history. If he looks at himself in the mirror he has to exercise some imagination to see through or separate himelf from the various social masks with which he is provided to live his life. An American does not have this sort of spiritual property. He can think of himself stark naked in the sight of God or of himself, if he wants to. But even so, if he looks in the mirror, whether he is wearing anything or not, he cannot help seeing the colourful, rather definite décor of his room and the clothing lying about in it. And there are plenty of hints and reminders of who he is that are subtler than the loud red striped pants on the chair and the star-spangled curtains.

A Canadian inevitably finds it hard to get as clear an image of himself as either a European or an American. Perhaps he does not own a mirror, or if he does it is a trick one. Certainly the masks of the various social roles from which he may choose are thin and few and ill defined. So too the demands of Canadian society are not much stronger than he decides to let them be. The well-groomed matron's glittering eye and throaty utterance, the bristling moustache and tenor bark of the regimental sergeant-major, long-practised instruments of communal survival for beleaguered settlements in a bleak land, sounded more formidable than they really were. The clumsy black skirts of M. Le Curé could not follow you far into the wilds of the bush or the city, if you chose to run free.

There is of course no lack of colour and variety in the images by which Canadians have presented their country to themselves and to the world. Totem poles and scarlet tunics, arctic char and Eskimo carvings, habitant bake ovens and dog carts, Gaelic Cape Breton and the bluenose quaintness of Peggy's Cove, Canadian

Club, the Klondike, the Calgary Stampede and half the world's fresh water lakes to fish in, the heights of Telegraph Hill and the Citadel, Queenston and Mount Royal, Banff and Grouse Mountain: these are the tourist images, telling little more about the realities of a complex urban society than our official emblem, the trembling leaf, or our authorized animal, a toothy industrious paddle-tailed giant rat. They are not necessarily untrue, or even spoiled by self-consciousness and overuse. But to evoke better the rich, incoherent variety of Canada's past and present, a simpler method will serve. Name the very place names, and even a random selection will afford a wild, extravagant mixture, redolent of things French and Irish and Indian, Eskimo, Icelandic and British, of human encounters and animals, of the experience of geography and climate, and of a history that stretches back four centuries to those first European habitations at St. John's in the 1540s, to the discoveries of Cabot and Cartier, and to the prehistoric past of the original Canadians. Besides the names of all the predictable British royal persons and ministers of the crown, besides all the explorers and missionaries of New France, one can find by the thousand such gloriously improbable places as Pugwash and Moose Jaw, Squamish and Spuzzum, Oka and Oba and Les Hauteurs de Rimouski, Povungnituk and Reykjavik, Snag and Destruction Bay, Placentia and Heart's Content, Harbour Grace and Come-By-Chance, the Niagara parish of Homer Virgil and MacNab, the uneasy biculturalism of St. Calixte de Kilkenny and Ste. Pudentienne de Roxton Pond. In the parliaments of Canada, members sit for places as richly named as Kamloops and Medicine Hat, Queens-Lunenburg and Trinity-Conception, Saskatoon and St. Louis du Ha! Ha!, Restigouche-Madawaska and Okanagan-Revelstoke, Okanagan Boundary and The Battlefords and Gaspé and Joliette-l'Assomption-Montcalm. The most prophylactic and homogenized of suburbs rejoice in names as unmistakably particular as Toronto Eglinton, Vancouver Quadra, Coast-Capilano and Montreal Jacques-Cartier-LaSalle. The riding of Iles-de-la-Madeleine consists of a few dots of land lost in the two-hundred-mile width of the Gulf of St. Lawrence; that of Mackenzie River is 150,000 square miles of snow between the Yukon and the magnetic pole.

The Canadians who lived in these places in the past century or more have invented, among other things, insulin and ice hockey, the telephone and standard time, Marquis wheat and McIntosh apples and a new kind of metropolitan government, the cobalt bomb and the first Atlantic steamship, the modern Commonwealth and the UN peacekeeping force. They have given the world a variety of great men from Dr. Norman Bethune, the most celebrated Western hero in Red China, to Paul-Emile Cardinal Léger, one of the leading liberals of Vatican II; two great modern critics of literature and culture, Northrop Frye and Marshall McLuhan; creative artists with the genius of Jean-Paul Riopelle and Duncan Macpherson and Norman McLaren, Stephen Leacock and Morley Callaghan and Gabrielle Roy; performers of the calibre of Glenn Gould and Maureen Forrester and Christopher Plummer. Since 1950 Canada has exported ballerinas to the New York City Ballet and Sadler's Wells, leading singers to the Metropolitan Opera and Covent Garden, half a dozen of the best drama producers on British television, five of the heads of the top eight or ten design and planning schools in American universities. Canadian engineers and scientists and doctors and missionaries have gone abroad by the hundreds in the twentieth century. And a million Canadians have spent from one to ten years overseas at war because Belgium and Poland and Korea were invaded.

Perhaps more than any other large country, Canada has been a place for people to come to, as well as to leave. Among the millions who have chosen to be Canadians are the doctors Hans Selye and Wilder Penfield, the sociologist Kaspar Naegele, the film maker Harry Horner, the opera director Herman Geiger-Torel, the arts administrator Peter Dwyer, the planners Stewart Bates and Hans Blumenfeld and a great company of brilliant men who have given the best part of their mature lives to this country. Among the sojourners who worked for a time in Canada, there have been the novelists Brian Moore, Malcolm Lowry and Ernest Hemingway, the conductors Zubin Mehta, Seiji Ozawa and Heinz Unger, the philosophers Jacques Maritain and Etienne Gilson, Ernest Rutherford who split the atom and radar's inventor Robert Watson-Watt, General Wycliffe Booth of the Salvation Army and Donald Coggan, Archbishop of York, John Grierson of the National Film Board and Michael Langham of Stratford.

The history of Canada is the heritage of all these men and what they have done here. Canada has been the home of Lord Strathcona and Louis Riel, Lionel Groulx and T. T. Shields, Harry Oakes and Gilbert LaBine, Marion Hilliard and Madame Vanier, Petra Burka and Yousuf Karsh, Garfield Weston and Lucien Rivard, E. P. Taylor, K. C. Irving, and J. C. Parkin,

Vilhjalmur Stefansson, A. Y. Jackson, Archibald The Arctic and Amor de Cosmos, Robert Service and Robertson Davies, Mordecai Richler and Mazo de la Roche, Mavor Moore and Marilyn Bell, Irving Layton and J. R. Mutchmor, Phil Gaglardi and Billy Bishop, "Punch" Dickins and "Wacky" Bennett, Allan Fleming, Alan Jarvis and Donald Fleming, Claude Jodoin, Claude Jutra and Claude Bissell, Tom Longboat, Donald Creighton and Oscar Peterson, Donald Gordon, Pauline Johnson, Fred Gardiner, Thomson of Fleet, and Chief Walking Buffalo of MRA, Tommy Burns, Norman Robertson, Rocket Richard, George Drew, Johnny Wayne, Joey Smallwood, Hartland Molson, Réal Caouette, Paul Anka and Vincent Massey.

Such names are already embedded in one or more of the undefined dialects and folklores which abound in Canada. Some day they may be common ground, part of one huge rich myth and common language.

The book that follows here is a brief and partial account of the history that has made them possible, and which they share with each other and with all their countrymen. At the end, turning from story to statement, there is a short description of certain qualities that can even now be identified as uniquely and peculiarly Canadian. But for signs and symbols, images and icons of who and what we are, one can scarcely do better than turn again to the contemplation of persons and to the willed and loving understanding of what they have done. Ned Pratt from the outports of Newfoundland, great heart and simple soul, epic giver of apocalyptic dinners (both in real life and in verse), one of the few major narrative poets of his age; Harold Town, painter, autobiographer and talker, who has never spent more than a few hours outside Toronto in his life, a master of seeing and of seven media in the visual arts; Gilles Vigneault of Natashquan on the North Shore a thousand miles oceanwards from Montreal, poet, chansonnier troubadour, celebrant of the French-Canadian nation; André Laurendeau, editor and playwright, royal commissioner extraordinary and one-time nationalist leader in the Quebec assembly; Anne Hébert and Micheline Beauchemin, Kate Reid and Emily Carr, Harry Somers, Hugh MacLennan, Michael Snow and Max Ferguson, Paul-Emile Borduas, Marius Barbeau, Marcel Dubé and Jean Le Moyne – they could only have happened in Canada. Because they did is perhaps the best reason of all for there being such an absurd and beautiful country as this one, and why July first, 1867, will always be a birthday worth celebrating.

1867
1914

1 THE BIRTH OF A NATION LIKE NO OTHER

They met for five days in Charlottetown in September and for three weeks in Quebec a month later. Many of them had never seen each other before. Others knew each other all too well, as bitter political enemies. They were men of two races, five provinces, and several political persuasions. Yet in that early fall of 1864 the little group of leaders from across British North America worked out the federal structure that made Canada possible, and found in each other the mutual trust to go back to their colonies and begin the struggle that made it happen. One legislator remarked that if anyone had predicted the nature of the meetings and the names of the delegates a few months earlier he would have been thought mad. Now, perhaps, it was the politicians who were a little mad.

Do not be deceived by their pictures – the stolid, mournful suits and the black chimney hats, the heavy black boots, the watch chains and the whiskers, the long faces and the stiff pose for the Victorian photographer. The fathers of our country were young men, as political leaders go, in their mid-forties most of them, born in the nineteenth century like every prime minister of Canada during the next hundred years. But more important than their primal vigour, they were speaking and acting like men possessed. They had been seized by a sense of urgency, by depths of conviction and passion that their sober countrymen have rarely felt since and need to feel again.

Deadlock, their familiar enemy, still mocked them and made them despair of any mere colonial solutions to the riddle of their political frustrations. Beyond their borders, it became clearer every day that the slightest change in the imperial designs of the United States or Great Britain could obliterate every goal they had spent their lives and hopes on.

They had reached a crisis in their affairs at home and were beset by a crisis in the affairs of the world around them. "We cannot go back. We cannot stand still," said one. "Events stronger than advocacy, events stronger than men, like the fire behind the invisible writing" stood plain before them and moved them to action. They felt the presence of "a thing at this moment almost forced upon us." They responded not with despair but with a dream and the courage to believe it could be made real.

The dream was twofold: a vision of harmony between races in a new kind of national state; and a vision of vast empires of land brought together in unity to be made prosperous and filled with people. In spite of the practical shrewdness of its believers and the laconic legal prose of their resolutions, the dream was a cousin of that Peaceable Kingdom which man in his extremities has glimpsed now and again on his trip outward from Eden on a few of history's clearer days.

Listen to the voice of French Canada, words taken from a speech made by its chieftain, Cartier.

Shall we be content to remain separate – shall we be content with a mere provincial existence – when, by combining, we could become a great nation? We will form a new nationality, a political nation, with which neither the national origin nor the religion of any individual can interfere. We are placed beside each other like great families. We are of different races not for the purpose of frustrating or warring against each other, but so that each by his efforts may compete and strive to excel the other and thus increase the prosperity and glory of all. The Catholic leaders of French Canada favour the new Confederation not only because we see in it so much security for all we hold dear, but because it does justice to our Protestant fellow-subjects as well.

Listen to the reply that came from the other man whose position mattered most, George Brown of the *Globe*, the voice of Protestant Canada West and the

The Founding Fathers: their first meeting, held at Charlottetown in 1864, lasted five days.

arch-enemy of the French – until he saw beyond his principles, put aside his past, and joined his old enemies in their better common cause.

One hundred years have passed away since the conquest of Quebec, but here we sit, the children of victor and vanquished, all deliberating how a great people may be established on this continent. Here sit the representatives of a British population seeking justice and here sit the representatives of the French population discoursing in the French tongue whether and how we shall have it We are endeavouring to adjust amicably greater difficulties than have plunged other countries into all the horrors of civil war. We are striving to do peacefully what Holland and Belgium, Austria and Hungary, Denmark and Germany, Russia and Poland. could only accomplish by armed force. Have we not great cause of thankfulness that we have found a better way? Can the pages of history find a parallel?

The vision of a political nation made up of cultural nations inspired them, but the more material vision of size and potential wealth in this union of the northern half-continent was positively inebriating. The United States had grown westward from the Atlantic seaboard by a process of purchases and wars that lasted several generations. This new federation was not only larger, but was to take place all at once. Brown asked his audience in the crucial debates of 1865 to look at a map of America. "Mark that island (Newfoundland) commanding the mouth of the noble river. Cross to the mainland," he said, and as he touched on each of the eastern provinces in turn, he named a pair of European kingdoms it exceeded in size. Finally he asked them to let their thoughts take wing to the far Pacific, to British Columbia, "the land of golden promise," and declared he would not even speak of the "vast Indian territories that lie between, greater

than the whole soil of Russia" which could soon be opened up to civilization.

Alexander Galt, the financial wizard of Confederation, made the tax and subsidy adjustments seem reasonable, even alluring, to the watchful Maritimers. He predicted to the businessmen of Montreal that their old commercial empire of the northwest, built on the fur trade and the river systems of the St. Lawrence and the Saskatchewan, would rise again with the aid of a transcontinental government and a transcontinental railway. In the greater world, as the largest red patch on Britain's globe Canada would provide the imperial link between the two oceans that touched on Europe and the Far East.

Whether their words were grand or merely grandiose, the men who founded Canada spoke of their dream, but they did not write it down. There is no hint of it in the British North America Act. Like the resolutions of the Quebec Conference which it derives from, the Act is conservative in tone and commitment, and leaves the most important things to inference or to future history.

In one area it is specific. Its drafting was an essay in practical federalism, and it reflects the hard trading and bargaining of the various provincial majorities and minorities. The founding fathers had before them the example of a federation, based on the principle of states' rights, which had been torn by civil war. Their answer was to move as close to legislative union and a strong central authority as possible – far closer, in fact, than has ever been achieved in later Canadian history.

The Act made no reference to government of, for, and by the people, as an American president had done a few months earlier at Gettysburg. In stating simply that the executive power was vested in the Queen, it summed up a tradition of liberties and law as old as

Dawn of an era: in 1866 the Great Eastern *layed Newfoundland end of Trans-Atlantic cable.*

the Anglo-Saxon jury or Magna Carta and as new as the Canadian device of responsible government – with which the history of the modern Commonwealth had begun a decade and a half before. This instrument of government was, in fact, designed to protect and conserve, in a new federal form, an ancient European heritage. The other part of that heritage, French and Catholic, had been brought to America at the end of the Renaissance, nearly two centuries earlier, before France herself moved down a different path into the fires of revolution.

To draw up their constitution, the founding fathers had met, as was fitting, in Quebec, on the rock of the medieval walled city that dominates the river of Canada, the one clear entrance to the far interior of the continent, the ancient key to a continental empire. Quebec stood both for the conserving of a European heritage and for the vast proportions of a new northern version of the American dream. The Quebec Conference of 1864, however, was but the beginning. It took nearly three years more of difficult and subtle manoeuvring on several interlocking fronts to turn the plans made there into the Act confederating the first four provinces. It took another four years to arrange for the entry of British Columbia and the North-West Territories.

The politics of this union was a lesson in the art of the impossible, like much Canadian politics ever since. It was one thing to have visions while looking at a map. It was another to move physically throughout the territory that had been mapped. Few of the founding fathers had ever been to any of the other provinces even once. None of them had travelled across the face of their proposed and so-called country. Practically speaking, they could not do so, and apart from a handful of explorers by canoe and foot, nobody had ever tried. The colonies were separated by such barriers as a thousand-mile stretch of empty prairie, ranges of mountains and massive outcroppings of the world's most ancient rock, several billion trees, and a fair quantity of salt water. Their peoples scarcely knew each other. They saw far more of their immediate neighbours in the United States than of other British North Americans. They were in closer touch with the Mother Country than with each other. Visitors and trade and news came mostly from Europe by sea, or by rail through the United States. The Grand Trunk Railway, the main line of Canada in the new railway age, had its eastern terminal at Portland in the state of Maine. To get to Quebec itself from either Montreal or from the Maritimes, the very delegates to the 1864 Conference had to get off at Richmond in the Eastern Townships and take a side journey north.

It was George Brown, the tall, red-headed Grit with principles as prominent as the bones of his face, who made the first move. On the night of Tuesday, June 14, 1864, after the fall of yet another government, Brown sent through an intermediary to the defeated Conservative leader, John A. Macdonald, the astonishing news that he was willing to serve with his bitter rival in a coalition to achieve some form of British North American federation.

Macdonald had been about the last man to take the idea of Confederation seriously. The ablest practising politician in Canada, a "cabinet maker" by trade as he once called himself, he was not given to entertaining high principles or hypothetical schemes. But once Confederation was a real political objective, Macdonald immediately became its master spirit and presiding genius. "The ugly charm of his face," in his biographer's words, "with his big nose and genial sardonic smile," was everywhere. At the balls and bargaining sessions of the Quebec Conference, no social detail, no political stratagem, was too small for him. The daughter of one Maritime politician wrote in her diary, "I went to dinner and John A. sat beside me. What an old humbug he is! He brought me my dessert into the drawing room – the conundrum!" Macdonald's family tragedies made him relish all the more the delights of society and politics when they were manageable, and seek drunken oblivion when they were not. He was no orator, partly because he did not take the art or himself that seriously. He lacked the overwhelming presence and the democratic appeal of George Brown. It is possible to see him as a Disraeli to Brown's Gladstone.

Brown could stand only so much of Macdonald. He resigned from the cabinet within two years and went back to the usual bitter attacks in the columns of his newspaper, including the habit of printing a "sick" notice every time Macdonald got too friendly with the bottle. But Brown's support for Confederation remained steadfast, a pledge that a good number of Toronto businessmen and Ontario farmers would support it too.

Canada East was a more difficult proposition. Since it was to be a separate province, the large English-speaking minority who made up half the population of Montreal, Quebec City and the Eastern Townships

John A: in 1867, "his ugly charm was everywhere."

had to be persuaded that their position was secure. Galt and D'Arcy McGee, the poet and orator who was assassinated by a Fenian in 1868, laboured to convince them. But the man who took the greatest political risks was Georges-Etienne Cartier, a youthful follower of Papineau in the 1837 rebellion, who had returned from exile to find a new climate of racial equality and cooperation. Cartier had become wealthy as solicitor for the Grand Trunk Railway and senior partner in the political firm of Macdonald and Cartier. "The funniest little man," as the governor-general's lady described him, he sang in a high clear tenor and wrote *O Canada! mon pays*, a song that once bid fair to become the national anthem. Cartier's strong *Rouges* opponents, like many of his own allies, had grave forebodings about giving up their secure position of equality within the province of the United Canadas for submergence in something larger, unknown and predominantly English.

In response, Cartier did not stress constitutional guarantees for provincial and racial rights, but in effect asked French Canadians to make a threefold act of trust: in the English majority and its resolve to deal justly with them; in the idea of diversity within unity;

15

Howe of Nova Scotia: Down the Botheration Scheme!

size of Toronto in those days) with its five newspapers, its "flash-dressed" ladies and rakish, cigar-smoking lumber barons, cheerfully settled down to see what could be done about making money out of the proposition.

In Halifax with its naval traditions, its slow pace and Georgian buildings ("less like a town than the debris of an old one for sale"), the old tribune of Nova Scotia, Joseph Howe, was busy denouncing "The Botheration Scheme." That proud, near-island province, still the world's fourth maritime power in the declining days of wind and wooden ships, felt closer in spirit and desire to the Mother Country than to Canada, a vulgar, little-known place locked in the continental interior.

But Dr. Charles Tupper, the sturdy young premier, played skillfully for time, and although public opinion was running against Confederation, he was able to carry enough of his own Conservatives, along with a few opposition members, to get it through both houses of the legislature. The anti-confederates appealed in vain to Britain, where they found the colonial secretary as committed to Confederation as Tupper. In protest the Nova Scotian separatists swept the first federal and provincial elections of 1867, but they finally settled for new terms and the consolation that they had been sold up river for a slightly better price. As in the Canadas, the cause of Confederation in Nova Scotia rested heavily on the support of church leaders like the young Presbyterian minister George Grant, later to be principal of Queen's and the greatest of Canada's university leaders.

The movement for Confederation was a triumph of political engineering executed from the top by a few committed men. But it was also an example, from Nova Scotia to Canada West, of courageous leaders asking their people to take the risks that changing times and a bold idea demanded. The guns and the church bells, the sky-rockets and the bonfires, the sermons and the front page salutes of Dominion Day, 1867, did represent a new stirring of public consent.

At Ottawa the precarious nature of the thing consented to could be grasped in a glance. High on a hill on the edge of the Pre-Cambrian Shield, surrounded by the shacks and stores and boarding houses of a frontier lumber town, overlooking a river full of logs and chips and sawdust, stood the imposing Gothic structure of the new parliament buildings – "the noblest piece of architecture in America," said Trollope – their towers rising against the horizon of the northern wilderness.

in themselves and their own ability to make these wishes respected within a federal government. He won the hesitant clergy to the cause of Confederation, and early in 1867 he and McGee made a final insurance trip to Rome, which was followed by strong declarations of support from the Canadian bishops.

Only in New Brunswick was Confederation put to the test of a general election and there, in spite of the promise of an intercolonial railway, it was defeated. To reverse that decision it took the failure of the anti-confederates' plans for commercial links with the U.S.; a governor conniving against his chief minister in order to precipitate another election; a forty-thousand-dollar campaign fund from Macdonald to buy votes at ten dollars a head; and the coincidental presence of a mob of Fenians on the American border threatening to "liberate" New Brunswick from British rule. In 1866 Confederation was accepted as the best choice left, and the thriving seaport of Saint John (near the

1866: A Georgian mansion in Toronto. The ritual of afternoon tea interrupts croquet.

LIFE IN THE CONFEDERATION YEARS

For the well-to-do, and they were many, life was uncommonly pleasant; for the very poor, and they were legion, existence was unbearably harsh. To be found drunk on the street appeared to be the privilege of the impoverished: in 1867, the Toronto *Globe* reported with astonishment the rare case of a man picked up on Queen "in a beastly state of intoxication," and yet carrying one hundred and forty pounds on his person. That same month a nine-year-old boy and a three-year-old girl were charged in police court with vagrancy: the boy was jailed for a month. At the other end of the social scale, the week was a cheerful round of conversazione-musicales, garrison theatricals, military balls, visiting opera troupes, earnest lectures ("What Will the World Come To?"), sedentary pursuits like croquet, and of course those regular afternoon fashion parades on the main streets.

1871: An artist for the Illustrated News *portrays a public flogging, Toronto jail.*

Hoop skirt and chignon usher in a new nation

The age of steel coincided with the dawn of Canadian nationhood. The Crystal Palace, built in 1851, and, of course, the hoop skirt were among the wonders of the world. Dress was so gargantuan that some fashionable ladies couldn't enter buses or walk abreast on the street. As for their hair—they braided it, tucked it up, folded it and curled it. But never in their wildest moments did they consider cutting it.

Elaborately embroidered, hooped "walking dresses" were fashionable in 1870.

It is hard to believe that the ladies of the Confederation years ever entered the water in what the Illustrated News *called "bathing toilettes."*

Winters were much harsher in Canada a century ago. Snow-clearing equipment was almost unknown. So were heated vehicles. The sleigh above was Montreal's version of winter street-car service in the 1870s.

Snowshoeing was the favourite winter pastime among the society blades and belles of eastern Canada. It permitted a degree of mild spooning.

Wild Indian shows vied with minstrel shows among travelling entertainments.

Advertising's naive and carefree childhood

The newspaper ads of 1867 tell more about everyday life than many a scholarly book. The style was pre-Madison Avenue, as were the brand names. Take for example, the "delightful preparation" known as *Odous Kallunterios*. "Don't let the name frighten you," the copywriter advised. "Ask for the *Tooth Embellisher* if the Greek title is unpronouncable." In those days there were no curbs on hyperbole. Professor McCauley, "the Prince of the Corn Curers," could blandly announce the discovery of the Philosopher's Stone while Humphrey's Homeopathic Specifics could promise to remedy everything from Salt Rheum to epilepsy. Since bargaining was common, there were few fixed prices, many goods being listed as "very cheap" or "good value." Liquor went at bargain rates. One Christmas case containing six bottles of wine and six of assorted spirits was listed at ten dollars, which may explain why the help wanted ads kept insisting that applicants be "sober and steady." In 1867 an importer could advertise for sale three hundred ounces of morphine and two hundred pounds of the finest Turkish opium. Such ads are as obsolete as those for snuff, sleigh bells and bagatelle boards. But the copywriter for the Mammoth Store sounds almost modern in his advertisement of July 20, 1867, for "Kool linen koats, kalkulated to keep everybody komfortable and kontent." The ad then went on to explain that all those missing Cs had been used up "writing down Coalition and writing up Confederation."

2 WINNING THE WESTERN EMPIRE

In 1867 the U.S. secretary of state told a Boston audience that Nature had designed the entire continent to fall, sooner or later, within the magic circle of the American Union. Of a bill before congress to admit British North America in the form of four states and three territories, the New York *Post* said that Americans had only to place an open basket under the tree and the ripe fruit would fall. It was a fair assumption. For nearly a century, the continental lands to the south and west of the Republic had one by one been engulfed as the tide of American settlement reached them.

Exhausted by civil war, most Americans were content to let Nature take her own good time in consummating the inevitable. It was left to an army of Fenian war veterans to push forward the day of reckoning. In the spring of 1866 they assembled in northern Maine for the liberation of New Brunswick, but their nerve failed at the sight of the eighty-one-gun Halifax flagship patrolling the waters off Eastport, roofing the bay with a cloud of black smoke. To the west, on May thirty-first, fifteen hundred Fenians crossed the Niagara River, with help from the border population, under the benevolently neutral eye of an American gunboat crew. "WAR. Revolution in Canada," blared the New York *Herald* on the second of June. "Give the Fenians a foothold for twenty days and their little detachment of occupation may be swelled into an army."

Toronto went wild with rumour and excitement. It brought back the days of the border raids after the 1837 rebellion. Veterans of 1812 recalled the glories of Queenston Heights and Lundy's Lane, and, more grimly, the American occupation of their capital and the burning of the parliament buildings. Old Bishop Strachan, who had threatened the invading general on the spot with the avenging wrath of Britannia and Almighty God, was still alive, a talisman of courage and the symbol of a military outpost's ancient resist-

ance to the vulgar bullying of Yankee democracy. The first weekend in June was spent in an agony of suspense. Six hundred volunteers of the Queen's Own Rifles were rushed across Lake Ontario by paddle steamer to Port Dalhousie, and from there towards the enemy by train. Unaware that the Fenians had not been reinforced and would soon have to retire, the Queen's Own attacked and pursued them immediately, and at Ridgeway, by virtue of a gallantry and stupidity worthy of the best British military traditions of the day, snatched defeat in battle from the jaws of strategic victory at the cost of three dozen casualties. The solemn half-mile-long military funeral procession through the streets of the city was one of the memorable public events of the century for the citizens of Toronto. "The autonomy of British America," wrote the *Globe*, was now "cemented by blood shed in battle."

Just to remind Lower Canadians that their history of American invasion stretched back to 1776 and to the French militia victory of Chateauguay in 1813, the Fenians again in 1870, under the same discharged Union Army colonel, organized a brief raid on the province of Quebec. Thus did the quixotic delusions of Irish patriots, the pathetic savings of Irish chambermaids, and the stance of American politicians willing to use or unwilling to offend Irish voters and bellicose editors provide the ultimate emotional stimulant for the founding of the Dominion of Canada.

If raids on the established provinces were the one sure way to guarantee that they would not become part of Nature's American plan for the continent, the likelihood of American occupation of the North-West Territories was another matter entirely. A thousand miles from the settlements of Canada West, over some of the bleakest terrain in the world, they lay adjacent to the vigorous new state of Minnesota, where a

Mustered at Thorold, Ont., to repulse Fenian Raiders of 1866, officers bade their ladies adieu.

hungry pack of railway and land promoters was pressing congress to annex them. If history meant anything, it mattered little who had the formal title to the lands above the forty-ninth parallel; they would belong eventually to the people who could colonize and develop them. To win the west, in fact, was the greatest challenge the new Dominion faced. This would be the first real test of the founding fathers' dream.

The key to the North-West Territories was not the company that had governed it as a trading reserve for two hundred years, but the ten thousand people of its only major settlement. The British government was able to force the Hudson's Bay Company to yield the northwest to Canada, but unfortunately none of the parties concerned took the trouble to consult or inform the inhabitants, most of whom were the half-breed descendants of fur traders and their Indian wives. The primitive life of the Métis, as the French-speaking majority were called, was founded upon the stability and culture of their Catholic parishes and upon the adventure of their great annual buffalo hunt, which, with some casual fishing and farming, enabled them to live in a carefree, independent and sporadically prosperous fashion. What contact they had with the outside world was chiefly by the slow ox-drawn caravans of screeching wooden-wheeled Red River carts south to the thriving young American town of St. Paul.

In 1868 the Métis were afflicted with the worst

drought in living memory, and by rumours that their land was being sold to an alien power. A small advance party of Canadian merchants and farmers had already settled among them, led by the druggist and land speculator Dr. John Schultz, who also published a little newspaper, *The Nor'wester*, to advocate swift Canadian annexation. To live with Schultz in 1868 came a brilliant young Queen's graduate from Ottawa, the poet-founder of the Canada First movement, Charles Mair, who began sending home letters that were published in the Ontario farmers' daily bible, the Toronto *Globe*. They described the Métis as shiftless men and loose women, unworthy of their magnificent land, and urged Ontario boys to move out and select a farm site (with Dr. Schultz's help) in the rich broad lands of the Red River valley. Government by Schultz and his kind was not something the Métis looked forward to.

After the first Canadian road survey team arrived, the Métis in alarm formed their own government based on the communal discipline of their buffalo hunt. They sent a party out to step on the survey chain, marched into Fort Garry to wrest control from the moribund Company council, and when the Canadian governor-designate arrived, their horsemen were ready to escort him firmly back to the American border.

Their leader was an intense black-locked, olive-skinned young man named Louis Riel, who had been sent east for training in a Montreal seminary and had lived for a time in the United States. Riel made one fatal mistake, the summary trial and execution of a racial bigot and trouble-maker named Thomas Scott, an action Riel took to show Canada that he meant business and must be respected. Otherwise, he acted throughout the winter and spring of 1869-70 with the firmness and skill of a master politician, toward the single goal of forcing the Canadian government to protect his people's rights. He raised the Union Jack over Fort Garry and refused the proffered aid of American agents ready to make the colony their protectorate. To deal with Riel, Ottawa sent out the Hudson's Bay Company's chief man in Canada, the canny Donald Smith. But in spite of Smith's eloquence, his judicious use of cash bribes, and his relation by marriage to Scottish half-breeds in the colony, Riel held the colony firmly behind him until spring. The government of Canada was forced to create not a territory but a province, in the Manitoba Act of 1870, with guarantees for French schools and the French language. The one thing Riel neglected was to procure an amnesty for himself. Mair and Schultz, whom he had jailed when they plotted an uprising against him, escaped back to Ontario and there aroused public opinion to force the despatch of a military expedition.

When the troops arrived on August twenty-third after their hazardous summer's trek through the wilderness, the founder of Manitoba slipped away into American exile. In his people's eyes, he became the first French-Canadian victim of Unionjackery, and of the higher righteousness and expansive ambitions of Protestant Ontario.

Though he was elected *in absentia* to parliament and was smuggled secretly into Ottawa to sign his name on the register of the House of Commons, Riel's presence was not for many years officially tolerated in Canada. He did spend several months under an assumed name in a Quebec insane asylum before settling permanently in the U.S. and becoming an American citizen. In 1885 he was summoned to lead the Métis again in the desperate rebellion on the North Saskatchewan, for which he was caught and hanged in the fall of 1885. But at that point the tragedy of Riel mingled with the epic of the building of a railway.

To reach the Pacific, Canada had to annex a colony half way across an empty continent from Red River and unlike any other place in the Dominion. British Columbia began as a gold rush community – saloons

The B.C. gold camps boomed again as the railway thrust forward. The camp is Yale; the year 1880.

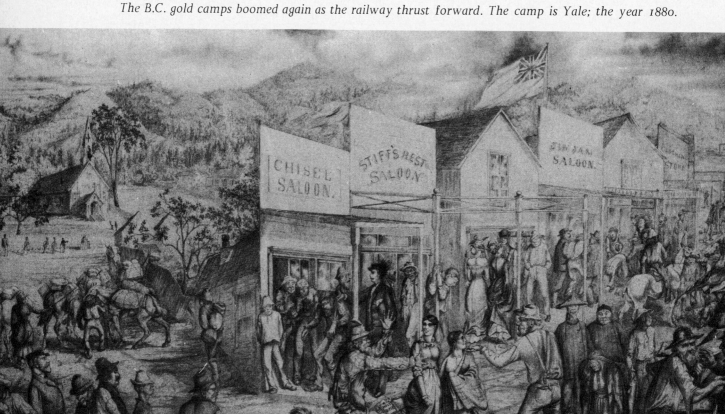

and sternwheelers, inflammable frame hotels and business done in gold dust and coins no smaller than one bit. After the gold was scooped off the mountainsides and streambeds, the farms and sawmills that had been started to supply the miners were left as the mainstay of a precarious economy. Yet the mild climate, the giant rain forest, the ocean-lapped, lotus-eating coast, the remote mountain valleys where fruit could be grown of legendary size and melons fed to the pigs, gave promise of paradisal wealth and ease.

The Englishmen of Victoria and the Island, with a wilderness estate or a government job, receiving their *Times* and their remittances from home, were mostly content to remain colonials. Hustlers and merchants from booming San Francisco pressed for annexation to the United States, whose coastal steamers were the colony's link with the outside world. But in mainland settlements like Gastown (before it became Vancouver) there were ambitious men from Canada who wanted to make the colony a Canadian province. One of their allies in Victoria was the editor of the *British Colonist*, a Nova Scotian who had had his name changed from Smith to Amor de Cosmos (Lover of the Universe) by Act of the California Legislature (nearly amended to Amor de Bacchus in the passing). Destined to be premier of British Columbia and a federal member of parliament, he was merely one of the most captious and unpredictable of the "queer kittle-kattle" the governor had to deal with. Theirs was, however, the cause of responsible government and Confederation. So with Britain's blessing, delegates were sent to Ottawa. They returned triumphantly with a Canadian commitment to take over the colony's debt, to pretend British Columbia's population was four times its actual size for purposes of federal subsidy, and, at the initiative of Cartier, the astonishing promise to begin building a railway in two years and complete it within ten. British Columbia became a province in 1871.

When the Liberal opposition in parliament caught Macdonald and Cartier taking $350,000 in party campaign funds from the promoters of the Pacific railway company, the ensuing scandal brought down the government and gave the Liberals under Alexander Mackenzie a five-year term of office. It was said of the earnest and intelligent new prime minister that if his chief virtue was that he had been a Baptist stonemason, his chief fault lay in his being one still. He had the bad luck to take office in 1873, the year a world depression set in, and, with frugal common sense, he proposed to build the railway piecemeal, as and when

Amor de Cosmos, premier of B.C.: Coolies, go home!

the government could afford to pay for it. But bad luck and common sense would not make Canada a nation.

With British Columbia threatening secession, and eastern Canada looking for a way out of the doldrums of the depression, the Liberals were turned out in the 1878 election in favour of Sir John A. Macdonald and a policy of tariff protection and national development. Macdonald believed that the railway had to be built, every mile of it on Canadian soil, and that it must be built soon if Canada was to populate the west and maintain its sovereignty there.

There was still doubt as to whether it could be done at all. The prospect of the uncharted Rockies and the muskeg and rock of the Pre-Cambrian wilderness north of Lake Superior tended to divide opinion between those who said it could never be done and those who said that, if it could, it would be ruinously expensive. Macdonald's opposition demanded the use of American routes over the most difficult parts. His own supporters wavered. American railway promoters foresaw the day when western Canada would be their profitable hinterland, reached by a series of spur lines from the south. British financiers, many of them committed to the old Grand Trunk Railway of eastern Canada and the United States, were either hostile or indifferent.

Macdonald found his men in George Stephen, the

suave and autocratic president of the Bank of Mont-real, and Donald Smith, his old envoy to Red River, who had already got control of an American railroad with a feeder line running north to Winnipeg. The new charter's terms were generous; a cash subsidy of twenty-five million dollars, twenty-five million acres of land, and such privileges as a monopoly of western traffic for twenty years.

At first all went well. There was a break in the depression between 1880 and 1882. Thousands of homesteaders flocked to Manitoba. Winnipeg, for the first time, became a boom town. With well-drilled efficiency, at remarkable speeds of four and five miles a day, the rugged general manager, William Van Horne, drove his army of construction men westward over the gently rolling prairies until by the end of 1882 the line was complete from the lakehead to the foot-hills of the Rocky Mountains.

To speed construction and to close out the hinter-land of western Canada from possible American rivals, the builders of the CPR took grave risks. They ran the line along the forbidding indented headlands of Lake Superior's north shore. They committed themselves to a southerly route through the Rockies a full year before Major Rogers discovered the pass through the Selkirk range that would make it possible to get through the mountain barrier at all. On the prairies the graders were sometimes only a few miles behind the surveying teams.

Then the great depression set in again, just as the difficult construction began. Track and locomotives disappeared into the muskeg between Sudbury and Schreiber. Limbs were lost by frostbite and dynamite; lives by rockfall and exposure, disease and exhaustion. Van Horne staved off mutiny and rioting when the pay car was months late. The Liberals lost no oppor-tunity to denounce the folly of attempting to build a railway through that "sea of mountains." Mac-donald's own Conservative supporters from Quebec and the Maritimes squeezed him for blackmail in the form of increased provincial subsidies and more local railways. In New York and London the American rail-ways and the Grand Trunk conducted a campaign to shake the confidence of potential investors. Men with sandwich boards denouncing the scheme appeared out-side the office where CPR bonds were sold in London.

No longer shrewd businessmen playing the short odds but visionaries committed beyond all sense, Smith and Stephen poured everything they had into the rail-road. They agreed that if it went down they must not

be found with a penny left in their pockets. When the final crisis came the only resource left was the Ca-nadian nation itself. Early in 1885 the company needed yet another round of government aid to save it from bankruptcy. But Macdonald despaired of carrying his own supporters in parliament, let alone the country. It seemed almost certain now that the opposition – in Ottawa and London and New York – had been right after all. The very idea of a transcontinental railroad, and perhaps too the very idea of Macdonald's Canada, had been a gigantic mistake. By February Macdonald could see no way out. He could do little but hedge and delay, yet he refused to give up hope. Smith and Stephen, with no idea what they would do by spring, somehow managed to stave off ruin with promises and desperate expedients. Then in March of 1885 Louis Riel took command of an Indian and Métis rising in the northwest, and unwittingly saved the day for the Canadian Pacific. Van Horne moved the Canadian militia from Ottawa to Winnipeg, sometimes laying track in front of them as they went, or ferrying them across lake inlets past uncompleted stretches. The trek that had taken two months in 1870 this time took only six days. Within another week, the first national military force in Canada's history was marching north in three columns from points along the railroad to-wards the centre of the uprising on the North Sas-katchewan River.

Without the CPR, Riel might possibly have founded a half-caste Haiti of the northwest, holding out for a few years until the Americans chose to help Canada extinguish it, or to take it themselves. British Columbia might well have seceded. At it was, the loan to com-plete the railroad passed parliament easily. Donald Smith tapped in the last spike, deep in the mountains of British Columbia at Craigellachie, on November seventh, 1885. A week later, in the North West Mounted Police compound in Regina, Louis Riel was hanged by the neck until he was dead.

Before his death in 1873 Cartier had hoped that the old tradition of the voyageur and the explorer, joined with that of the Métis, might inspire his people to plant French culture beside English along the Sas-katchewan and the Red, as it was on the St. Lawrence. But French Canada withdrew into itself. And the same expansive English-Canadian nationalism that enabled Macdonald to drive the railway westwards to the last spike drove the troops, too, to catch and kill the man who became the symbol of French Canada's right to survive.

26

LOUIS RIEL

PRAIRIE PROPHET

The "prophet on horseback," as his American biographer calls him, remains to most of his countrymen an uncomfortable conundrum. He is hero, statesman, martyr, madman, rebel, traitor, visionary and genius rolled into one. A Catholic mystic, he defied his church. A revolutionary, he eschewed battle. A member of parliament, he could not take his seat. Had he been as militant as his great general, Gabriel Dumont (seen at the extreme right in the above drawing), he might have carved a unique semi-primitive nation out of the heart of North America. For, though he was only one-eighth Montagnais, Louis "David" Riel made himself spiritual and political leader of the great buffalo-hunting nation of mixed-bloods, or Métis. At the very least he deserved to be remembered as the Father of Manitoba; at the most as the Saviour of the West (from U.S. occupation). Ironically, his main legacy has been to the continuing and unresolved agony of the dual nation which, in his own agonized yet oddly courageous way, he helped to construct.

Fort Garry, the site of modern Winnipeg, was seat of Riel's government.

1870 UPRISING

Red River cart, a unique Métis development, preceded steam and rail era.

Specially built voyageur boats of Red River military expedition were portaged on rollers or toted on men's backs for hundreds of miles.

By 1870, Riel had made himself head of the provisional government of the "new nation" of Manitoba. The Canadian government as yet had no legal jurisdiction here, since it was former Hudson's Bay Company territory as yet unceded to the new Dominion. But Riel's execution of Thomas Scott, "a hot headed, irrepressible and irresponsible Orangeman" in one neutral observer's view, made the uprising seem like a Protestant-Catholic holy war. Orange Ontario, screaming for blood, put a five-thousand-dollar price on Riel's head. And although Ottawa and Riel had agreed to terms under which Manitoba would become part of Canada, a military expedition set off for the Red River country – four hundred British regulars and eight hundred green volunteers, mainly Orangemen from Ontario crying for revenge. This remarkable ninety-six-day military trek – one of history's most arduous – brought an end to Riel's government. The undisciplined troops, looting Fort Garry and Métis homes, caused far more casualties in a few weeks than Riel had in ten months. Some Métis leaders were hunted down and killed. But Riel escaped, was elected to parliament while in hiding and, helped by a five-thousand-dollar federal bribe, went into exile in the U.S., there to await a second call to leadership.

1885 WAR

Gatling, used against Métis, was world's first machine gun.

A different Riel, more mystic and mercurial, arrived in Saskatchewan to champion "the right of the people."

Gabriel Dumont, "prince of the prairie," whose word was law on the plains, ended up in a Wild West show.

When he returned to take up the Métis and Indian cause in Saskatchewan, Riel had been twice confined to mental asylums. But his general, Gabriel Dumont, was brilliantly sane. In a series of battles, two of them shown here, he and his allies fought British redcoats to a standstill. At Fish Creek, Dumont, supreme tactician of the famous buffalo hunt, treated his adversaries exactly as if they were animals, forcing them into a "pound" and peppering them with scrap iron. The regulars had not learned the century-old lesson of Bunker Hill and were still using close-order tactics against ungentlemanly native sharpshooters. A few days later, Chief Poundmaker successfully pitted his outnumbered Crees, armed with obsolete weapons, against a force of cannon, long range rifles and the new Gatling gun. The troops had sped to the scene via the half-finished CPR. In the end they beat Riel. But had he allowed Dumont's guerrillas to harass the railway at the outset, history might have taken a different course.

At Fish Creek, April 24, 1885, Dumont's sharpshooters in ravine easily picked off troops silhouetted above them.

At Cut Knife Creek, on May 2, Poundmaker's invisible Indians lured Col. Otter's troops into a three-sided trap.

1885 DEFEAT

OPPOSITE PAGE

Seven pound cannon saved troops from complete disaster at Cut Knife Creek, where Mounties also fought.

Defeated Indians were photographed in Regina at war's end. Eight were hanged.

Surrender of Poundmaker to Maj.-Gen. F. D. Middleton was painted on spot. He and Big Bear were jailed three years, and died broken in spirit.

The bearded figure in the photograph above (in the dock in a Regina courtroom) is talking his life away. Louis Riel is protesting his lawyer's plea of insanity – the only plea that can save him. And why? Because, "though it would be easier for me today to plead insanity . . . I have this satisfaction – that if I die I will not be reputed by all men as insane, as a lunatic!" Thus did The Prophet of the New World choose death before dishonour and give meaning to his crusade. Was he sane? Or was the rest of the nation insane? The government-appointed, politically oriented board found him sane enough to hang; and hang he did, on a chill November day at the hands of a crony of Thomas Scott, who whispered: "Louis Riel – you cannot escape from me today!" In a sense, then, Riel committed suicide. But so did the Conservative Party of John A. Macdonald, who refused to reprieve him – an action which seems politically insane in the light of subsequent events. The insanity of English-French bitterness, fed by Riel's trial and execution, still rages uncured eighty years after the fact.

3 THE HARD PATH TO CANADIANISM

On the Champ de Mars in Montreal the Sunday after Riel's death, an enormous crowd of French Canadians assembled to protest the judicial murder of their brother. Within a year the leading speaker at that meeting, Honoré Mercier, had achieved the very thing Cartier in 1867 had sought to avoid. By an appeal to French Catholic nationalism, Mercier formed a new political party, won the provincial election in 1886, and was sworn in as prime minister of Quebec. In response to Mercier's programme, D'Alton McCarthy, an Ontario Conservative once touted as Macdonald's successor, began a campaign against the very existence of French Canada as anything more than a vestigial ghetto within the province of Quebec. He and his associates set off an inflammatory newspaper war. "Either this country will be French or it will be English," he said. In 1890, Manitoba's answer was to legislate French Catholic separate schools out of existence, and Schultz, the Métis' old enemy, now lieutenant-governor, signed the bill that abolished the official use of the French language in his province.

"How long can the present fabric last? Can it last at all? These are questions which surge in my mind and to which dismal answers suggest themselves," wrote the new Liberal leader, Wilfrid Laurier. Not only racial antagonism, but all those centrifugal forces and separatisms which had been held in check for the founding of the Dominion and in the first generation of its history, now revived and roamed the land. Oliver Mowat, the premier of Ontario, relentlessly pursued the cause of provincial rights before the bar of Canada's final court of appeal in Britain. The electors of Nova Scotia in 1886 returned a provincial government which had campaigned on the drastic promise to seek separation from Canada. If Gladstone was prepared to give his life to the repeal of Britain's union with Ireland, why should he not repeal the more recent union Act of

1867 and grant Home Rule to a Canadian province as well?

Brooding over all the troubles of Canada and inhibiting every enterprise hung the last and darkest years of the great world depression. The little wood-burning CPR engines with their fat smokestacks and cow-catcher prows escorted their short processions of carriages through lonely railway settlements. The track was the skeleton of a country and a people who were not yet there. Even some of the first homesteads in more settled regions of Manitoba were now abandoned. A million people left Canada for the United States in the decade before 1891, and in that year one native Canadian in five was living south of the border. Young men from the Maritimes left to make their fortunes in "the Boston states." French Canadians did not migrate west, but rather to the milltowns of industrial New England. Though the industries of central Canada had benefited from the captive markets provided by Macdonald's National Policy of tariff protection, there were empty houses in every Ontario town in the early 1890s. The Dominion which had "begun in Lamentations seemed to be ending in Exodus," said the former Liberal finance minister, Richard Cartwright. As his party's solution to the ills of Canada, he proposed commercial union with the United States, a policy that had brought prosperity to British North America before 1867. Some people, like the editor of the Toronto *Globe*, and Goldwin Smith, the most brilliant of the English-Canadian intellectuals, frankly welcomed the idea of free trade as the first step towards political annexation and the end of an experiment that had failed.

In spite of all the nation's troubles, the Conservatives managed to eke out their fourth successive victory in the federal elections of 1891. They did it, with an assist from some stolen galley proofs, by identify-

LAYING OUT THE GRIT CAMPAIGN.

Tory campaign poster for 1891 election showed Liberals as American puppets. Tories won.

ing Liberals with Yankees, and themselves with the British tradition. The influence and money of the CPR were freely spent to help them. But it was above all the victory of one man over the immediate temper of his times.

John A. Macdonald had become the embodiment not only of his government and his party but of Canada itself. The chief architect of Confederation, its sustainer and builder for a quarter of a century, he could still, in spite of all trends and evidence to the contrary, somehow convince, cajole, inspire, and when necessary corrupt his countrymen into believing and acting as if the creation of a new kind of American nation in the northern half of the continent was possible.

The last but one of the Fathers of Confederation still active in politics, a parliamentarian for nearly half a century, Macdonald at seventy-six had become a myth in his own lifetime. Gallant and humorous on the brink of ruin, gambler, opportunist, prince of misrule, a Figaro who knew within the limits how to cope with a British lord, he was the hero most Canadians secretly wished to be, even though they knew perfectly well that the Liberals, with their reason and their rectitude, were what they chiefly resembled.

"When this man is gone who will then take his place?" asked Goldwin Smith. "What shepherd is there who knows the sheep, or whose voice the sheep

know? Who else could make Orangemen vote for Papists or induce half the members for Ontario to help in levying on their own province the necessary blackmail for Quebec? Yet this is the work which will have to be done if a general break-up is to be averted. Things will not hold together of themselves."

"You'll never die, John A.," called the clear voice from the dark cavern of the rally hall. Die he did, still prime minister of Canada, a few weeks after carrying the lonely burden of the last campaign. Four Conservative successors struggled with the impossible, and failed. The last prop of the nation seemed gone.

Then the miracle happened. The year 1896 saw Canada's great reversal of fortune. The world depression lifted; Sir John and the dream of Confederation, both reborn, assumed the prime ministership in the person of Wilfrid Laurier, a member of the other party and the other founding race.

An orator and an intellectual, as courtly and elegant in manner as his gloves and silk hat and great white plume of hair, lacking the least trace of that vulgarity that had made Macdonald better loved but less admired, Laurier nonetheless had Macdonald's magic personal charm, his easy cheerfulness, his gift for transcending angry opposites, and his love of leaving troubles for tomorrow. Laurier took over Macdonald's National Policy – western development, railway building, and, with the new twist of imperial

35

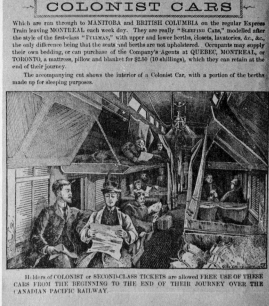

The noisiest immigration campaign ever, 1900-10, flooded Europe with pamphlets, posters, ads.

preference, tariff protection. He brought into his first cabinet Macdonald's old opponents, the Liberal premiers of Ontario and Nova Scotia. He convinced reluctant Ontario Protestants that a Papist blood brother of Riel was supremely fitted to be prime minister of Canada. Above all he persuaded French Canada that liberalism need not be another form of godlessness, as it often seemed in France. (Had not an Englishman said that Aquinas himself was the first Whig; and was not the Catholic Lord Acton, with his ideal of the plural, multiracial society, also the greatest liberal of his day and the most relevant for Canada?) Laurier called himself, both in pride and self-mockery, "*un Britisher.*" Besides his French classical education he had gone for two years to an English-speaking school, and had read law at McGill. As the *Rouge* he was, he could poke fun at the classical colleges as "hotbeds of conservatism." He firmly opposed the growing clerical and racial nationalism in Quebec. Like Cartier before him, he asked French Canadians to follow him in his act of commitment, not to a weakening of their own cultural nation but to a strengthening of the wider political nationality that was Canada.

It was during Laurier's first years in office that the world suddenly discovered Canada. The twenty-year fall in food prices dramatically reversed itself. Europe could no longer feed the growing numbers of her new industrial masses. As the American frontier came to an end, the vast empty lands of the Canadian prairies became the new west. The tide of settlement, so long expected, flooded in at last.

Clifford Sifton of Winnipeg, Laurier's powerful

minister of the interior, hunted Europe and America for the right settlers. He published pamphlets in twenty languages praising the soil of the Canadian prairie and the magnificent crops that could be grown there. In seven thousand American newspapers he advertised free homesteads for those who would come and work them. He sent agents to Hamburg to pick out "the sturdy peasants in their sheepskin coats" from among the prospective immigrants who crowded into the great port from central and eastern Europe. The younger sons of large English households could purchase ocean passages out of Liverpool for less than thirty dollars. The colonist cars from St. John to Winnipeg were jammed with passengers at six dollars a head. Every harvest time, young men from Ontario rode the rails west, and many of them stayed on to make their lives in the wheatlands.

In 1890 wheat had been an insignificant export. Twenty years later the very life of the Dominion seemed to hang on it. In the board rooms and brokerage houses of the east, men waited eagerly for the daily reports of the prophetess Cora Hind, who toured the west watching the crop grow, predicting from day to day the expected yield. Magazine readers had it put to them that the healthy way to take their wheat was puffed – THE WONDERS OF EXPLODED GRAIN – or on the contrary, that it should be Shredded or Whole. "Of course you should *Eat More Bread* and less meat for the sake of your health," ran an ad in *The Busy Man's Magazine.* By 1910 the Dominion Cerealist, Charles Saunders, was becoming famous for breeding his new fast-ripening Marquis wheat and was later knighted.

The west was suddenly the dominant new fact in the Canadian nation. Over a million settlers flooded in during Laurier's fifteen years in power. Saskatchewan and Alberta became provinces. Unemployment vanished in the east as the wheat boom summoned a new steel industry into existence, and brought a demand for all the building and farm and household supplies that Canadian factories could produce. A market for industrial stocks and bonds was created for the first time; two and a half billion dollars in foreign capital and even greater amounts of Canadian public and private funds poured into new enterprise. "The Cinderella of the western world," wrote a British visitor in 1906, "the poor relation has come into her fortune. A single decade has swept away all diffidence." An American lady journalist wrote in 1907, of My Canadian Conversion, "Canada is starting in housekeeping among the nations of the earth as if she had all the high djinns of Persia at her call."

Even Canadian bankers – the kind who only wanted to lend money when a borrower could prove he had no need for it – were moved. One of them on his first trip west in 1902 was astounded to see his fondest hopes exceeded: "Within four or five years every railroad in the country will have to double-track its line to handle the traffic." Laurier and his government caught the fever. They helped to build not one but two more transcontinental railways. The little town of Fort George, B.C., planned to have ten railways running into it. A scheme was afoot to run a railway north from Dawson City and from there through Alaska to make connections with Siberia. Wildest of all came the boom in land. "Saskatoon will be a city of four hundred thousand people," the real-estate sharks advertised in 1912. Town lots that are empty still were staked out and sold in the west at a hundred dollars a foot as the boom reached its climax.

The new gambling spirit of buoyant optimism had a second source. The century had begun with the news of a different golden harvest – in the Klondike. It did not matter that out of the hordes of men who set out for the Yukon, or the forty thousand who got there, only a few dozen ever became millionaires. The Klondike brought men and money into the country and a habit of taking wild risks and expecting an Eldorado. It set the tone of the period and gave a new word to the Canadian language.

In the end, of course, it all meant trouble. Short run trouble for the gamblers and the gulls when the boom collapsed in 1913, and permanent trouble, for which

Laurier: more admired, less loved than Macdonald.

Canadians have paid ever since, from rash investment in inefficient industry and unproductive land and unnecessary railways. But the people kept coming – four hundred thousand immigrants in 1913 alone. And most of them came to Canada to stay. As the war clouds darkened in Europe it was clear that Canada was, in Laurier's phrase, a young giant, and she had a part to play in the world.

Sir Wilfrid had charmed Queen Victoria at her Jubilee and was the darling of the English duchesses. But he firmly resisted Britain's attempts to make Canada an integral part of Empire. It was on the question of Empire that he ultimately met his downfall, for English-Canadian nationalism in his time, as never before or since, took the form of imperial pride.

The Boer War began the trouble. French Canadians saw the war as the heroic resistance of a dispossessed people, akin to the Métis, or at best the spending of blood and money on a doubtful foreign adventure. English Canadians saw a different war; they heard the call to the colours and cried shame on Laurier for failing to do more than equip and ship volunteers. After Laurier had further offended French-Canadian feeling

The Boer war: Canadian troops (here, in South Africa) helped win it. But Laurier went down.

by refusing to force the western provinces to guarantee French schools and language rights, the final blow came over his proposal for a Canadian navy.

In the 1911 elections he found himself proclaimed a traitor in both languages. "In Quebec I am branded as a Jingo, and in Ontario as a Separatist." He also had the misfortune to have accepted the excellent terms of a reciprocity treaty offered by the United States, to which the Conservatives responded by placarding their leader Borden's picture set in a Union Jack beside Laurier's in the Stars and Stripes. Sifton and eighteen leading Liberal businessmen deserted Laurier over reciprocity, and Borden captured Ontario handily. Laurier also lost his solid grip on Quebec, as the nationalists, led by the brilliant Henri Bourassa of *Le Devoir*, took twenty-seven seats there. He never returned to power.

Laurier once compared the fate of political man to that of Sisyphus; no sooner had a task been accomplished than it had to be performed all over again.

Nevertheless his very life, like Canada's survival, was a kind of victory; an accomplishment that could not be undone even if it would have to be renewed and repeated by others. No matter if Canada's century, as Laurier once called it, had lasted little more than a decade before the boom collapsed and war came to Europe. The country had now survived both rags and riches, both the despair of the lean years and the recklessness and folly of the fat. It had survived the temptations to be taken up into the larger imperial sphere of either Britain or the United States; and thanks to the ultimate moderation, magnanimity and commitment to Canada of Borden and Bourassa as well as Laurier, it had refused the easy path to dissolution.

Canada as she approached the completion of her first half century had made of survival itself a habit. She had withstood many tests. She faced next the sterner test of total war, and the end of the world in which she had been conceived as a nation.

"A peasant in a sheepskin coat," said Immigration Minister Sifton, "is good quality." The eight men in cloth coats are Russian peasants heading for western farms.

THE IMMIGRANTS

The ladies are all Scots, and all marked for domestic service. "Servant girls," a government ad of the '90s said, "are in great demand and command $8-12 a month."

The land was free: 160 acres in the fertile, empty west for any homesteader brash enough to take it and strong enough to work it. For many years, such men were rare. From 1881 to 1896, between Lake of the Woods and the Rocky Mountains, settlers took up only 56,000 homesteads and abandoned 16,000 of these. Then everything happened at once. A new prime minister, Laurier, and a new immigration minister, Sifton, took office just as the long depression broke. The CPR joined them in the noisiest campaign for immigrants that Canada has ever run. The number of newcomers who landed in 1897 – 32,000 – was twice the number who came in 1896. By 1911, two million more had followed. Well over a third came from the U.K., another third from the U.S., and almost all the rest from continental Europe. The bait Canada dangled was so bright that Germany lodged an official protest against "the attempt to lure our countrymen to this desolate sub-arctic region." For Galician peasants landed in Canada, the government paid the North Atlantic Trading Company a bonus – $2 each and $5 for the head of a family. A poor but independent man could take ship from Liverpool and land in Winnipeg for a shilling less than £11 – if he brought his own mattress. Many did; they peopled Canada.

The human tide

Three-quarters of the new-comers already spoke English. The rest were a rich mixture of the races of earth, although all but some CPR labourers had white skins. Half of them took root here; within a few years the other half had either drifted south or gone back home.

This family is English, and most of their working capital is in the arms and backs of the older children. Even so, a shack, cow, furniture and food will cost over £100. "All new settlers," a British report said, "especially women, must expect to rough it."

These young families from the steppes of Russia sailed in 1900 on the Lake Champlain, destined for Manitoba. To them, the prairie wheatlands sounded much like the land they knew. "A man," they were told, "can earn . . . the price of an acre of land a day."

Two generations of New Canadians, on shipboard. Both are Scottish.

Then there were the Doukhobors. During 1899, more than seven thousand reached Canada. By 1902 most were farming homesteads in Saskatchewan. But that year they began the protest marches, as above, that go on yet.

Galicia, the home of these dark men and pretty girls, was a province of the old Austro-Hungarian Empire. By 1914 more than 200,000 Galicians had settled in the Canadian west, most of them in sod houses.

From the harbour at Quebec City the through-passage immigrants were transferred by coach to the Grand Trunk Railway's passenger depot. Special "colonist" cars, with stoves for food and planks for beds, connected with CPR trains west. Journey took four days.

This is the steerage deck of the S.S. Lake Champlain. *The year is 1900, the next port Quebec City. Some ships were almost as full on return trip.*

Steerage passengers (these are aboard Lake Huron *in 1899) brought their own pots and pans, but cooked food supplied by the steamship company.*

West by train: this is what the inside of a "colonist" car looked like.

PRAIRIE SCHOONERS.
CANADIANS RETURNING
FROM U.S.A TO TAKE
UP LAND AT EDMONTON

How they reached
the land of hope

Then as now, there was a heavy flow of humanity back and forth across the U.S. border. These prairie schooners came to Alberta from Montana.

The railroads made immigration sound like showbusiness. These Americans, on their way to take up land outside Edmonton, told the world.

This is the last lap. A homesteader, his family and all their worldly goods make ready to leave Edmonton for the land they've staked to the north. This is 1907, and the great Alberta land rush is on.

When a man staked his future on the fertility of the soil, the day he broke the virgin prairie was the high point of his life. But for the cost, most men would have invited a photographer. This man paid it.

44

Grass and dirt
at the journey's end

For this family the end of the line and the beginning of a new kind of life was a grassland homestead near Lloydminster, Alta. Their home, and their cows', is mud brick. Their neighbours are beyond the horizon.

A few years before, this Galician family lived through an entire Saskatchewan winter in a sod hut that was more cave than house. The head of the family is now a leading member of the local Galician community. Soon two of his sons will be graduates in the professions. None of it came easily. "No man should emigrate to the northwest," said an early report, "who will not live and work hard."

1914

1945

4 THE LEGACY OF FLANDERS FIELDS

Nineteen hundred and fourteen was to be "Peace Year" at the Canadian National Exhibition. From the summer cottages of central Canada and from western homesteads set in horizons of ripening wheat, Canadians could look back on a half century of peace since the founding of the Dominion. Schoolboys bravely recited Pauline Johnson's "The Yankee to the south of us, Shall south of us remain," but real Yankee invasions were by now part of the distant past. British colonial wars were adventures you read about in Henty and Kipling and some day might run off to join, but they only served to underline the basic securities of Canadian life in 1914.

Before the CNE closed that year, German armies were smashing towards Paris and the taxis were out for the Battle of the Marne. Over a quarter of a million men were already dead. At least one graduating class of French high-school boys was far on its way towards total extermination. The raw recruits of the first Canadian Expeditionary Force were hastily assembling at Valcartier.

A quarter of the men who sailed on October first in the first contingent from Quebec would never return; some who were to sail again for Britain in the fall of 1939 would spend, Ulysses-like, a large part of their adult lives outside Canada. The half-million Canadians who went overseas in World War I, even if they were forunate enough to survive the mud and guns and gas of the years in the trenches, left behind a world they could not return to and would never know again..It was a world whose major divisions were between Europe and her colonies, Catholics and Protestants, masters and men, in which the difference between right and wrong was clearly known and there was an answer to every question, even if the approved answer was usually 'no'. The Great War that marked the mid-point of Canada's first hundred years brought with it the end of Canada's colonial childhood.

When Canadians were reading for the first time about those two spiritual sisters, Anne, in her green-gabled farmhouse on the red-soiled sea island farm, and Nellie McClung's twelve-year-old hired girl on the harsh flat Manitoba homestead, or about the characters on the main street of Stephen Leacock's little town in the sunshine, they were not necessarily indulging in nostalgia for bygone days. They recognized themselves and life as they knew it.

It was not that life was easy in 1914. Pain and sorrow and hard work were expected. A twelve-hour day was still common in industry; in 1913 three-quarters of a million men in North America were injured in industrial accidents, and twenty-five thousand killed. Life on the farm was a round of backbreaking labour. Modern technology, where it existed at all, was the clumsy steam-powered tractor and the threshing machine that resembled a dinosaur. Science looked more like the contraption of Kitty Hawk than the lines of a jet. Diphtheria and tuberculosis took an appalling toll of lives, and it was common for half the offspring of a family to die in childhood. Hospitals were places with high dingy ceilings and black doorknobs. In most places it was still the age of cardboard collars and horse serum, carbon street lamps, water pumped by hand and Saturday night baths heated on the stove.

Electric power had taken over street railways from the horses and city streets had grown a forest of poles and wires, but few people yet recognized electricity for the total revolutionary it was soon to be. The motorcar was a luxury to be brought out on Sundays in good weather. It was rarely legal to drive faster than fifteen miles an hour, and a motor league man wrote

48

This was the world of 1914: brave, happy and hopeful. It was to be "Peace Year" at the CNE.

hopefully of a distant Utopian day in which the motor-car, not the pedestrian or the horse, would have the right of way on the roads. Paving was still the exception. Most of Yonge Street in Toronto was a place where boys could sail boats in the gutter in spring and from which department stores delivered parcels by sleigh and dapple-grey horses in winter. The quiet certitudes of life in 1914, like its hardships and terrors, were familiar and could be taken for granted.

The war brought drastic social and economic change. Goods that once came from Europe had to be manufactured at home. And the men and women in the new factories had come to the cities to stay. For the first time the Canadian steel industry produced over half the nation's steel requirements. The smelting of base metals increased threefold. More than a billion dollars worth of munitions were produced in Canada during the war. One third of the shells used by the British armies on the western front were made in Can-

ada. British Columbia Sitka spruce flew over the battle-fields of France in the shape of the Jennies of the Royal Flying Corps.

To pay for it all and to organize it, the federal government assumed an entirely new role. The War Measures Act of 1914 gave the government dictatorial powers which were used in a manner that would have been unthinkable a few months before. And like the emancipation of women and the sudden new growth of urbanism, big government had come to stay. The first federal income tax, the huge national debt, the wheat board, a nationalized railway system, the National Research Council, and the 1918 Civil Service Act which ended patronage and put government work on a professional basis – all these were among the many wartime innovations that became permanent features of Canadian life.

The discovery that a colonial race of farmers and fishermen and suppliers of raw materials could acquire so quickly the skills to sustain an advanced industrial economy was exhilarating. A source of pride, too, was the battle record of men whose ingenuity and endurance and daring, tested already in their struggle with a harsh environment, made the Canadian Corps perhaps the most effective fighting force on the western front, and won for Billy Bishop and the other Canadian air aces the largest number of kills of any group of Allied flyers. Canada's five years at war gave her a new self-confidence and led, just as surely as Sam Hughes's rude disobedience to Kitchener's 'orders' for integrating Canadian troops in the British armies, to Canada's new role in world affairs after the war.

Nationalism born of war also had an ugly face. Naturalized Canadians with the misfortune to have been born in enemy lands lost their votes. A respected Liberal statesman declared that the war was a battle of "the Lower against the Higher, of the pagan against the Christian." The minister of finance said he would bankrupt Canada if necessary to save the Empire. Protestant churches on occasion turned their evening services into recruiting rallies complete with sergeants ready to enlist volunteers at the doors. Emancipated war goddesses roamed the streets ready to award a white feather to any man not on crutches who lacked a uniform. The Imperial war minister, Lord Kitchener, glared out from the recruiting posters and with an accusing finger passed judgment on the virility of any man who refused to serve him.

The war brought out the worst in English-Canadian arrogance toward French Canada. English was the language of command. French-speaking volunteers were not at first grouped into units of their own. The chief recruiting officer for Quebec City was a Methodist minister from Toronto; the troops on garrison duty there were English-speaking units. There was a French-Canadian tradition of military adventure as old as the first explorers and as recent as the thirty-five thousand volunteers who had fought in the American Civil War. But by 1916 recruiting in Quebec had fallen off drastically. A crowd marched into a recruiting rally and started a riot. When the courts sustained Ontario's law abolishing French-language instruction in the schools, French nationalist leaders called for a relief fund for the victims of the Prussians of Ontario.

As losses mounted on the western front, many English Canadians concluded that they must coerce French Canada into doing its fair share. Laurier, who had never wavered in his support of the war effort, warned that conscription would not yield worthwhile

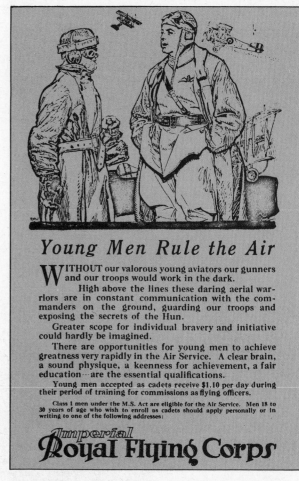

In 1917, the call to arms was sounding everywhere.

But in 1917, too, separatism was a hot issue in Quebec.

This is the victory parade in Namur, Belgium. Cavalry leads Canadian troops to an ovation.

results – quite correctly, as the widespread evasion and rioting of 1918 proved. Leading English-speaking Liberals nevertheless accepted Borden's invitation to join a coalition government to fight an election on the conscription issue in December of 1917. Laurier won all but three of Quebec's seats. The coalition swept the rest of the country. The bitterness over conscription left a scar that would take more than a generation to heal. It created a climate in which the most reactionary side of French nationalism could flourish, and in which French withdrawal and isolation, not only from the rest of Canada but from the world and from the twentieth century, might seem both attractive and possible.

The war was storing up other problems for the future of Canada. The wartime doubling of wheat acreage led to the cultivation of unsuitable land, and

to steep farm mortgages at inflation prices. An ambitious programme for the conservation of Canada's national resources had its budget cut in 1917 because it was not essential to the war effort, and the Conservation Commission disappeared three years later. The premature death of a first attempt to plan Canada's new towns and cities led to incalculable waste in their later growth.

The men returning after Armistice Day from the battle to make the world safe for democracy made high demands on the future. It is not surprising that 1919 was to be a year of great social unrest, and that the next decade was to be a time of rising nationalism. The men who had lived and fought together overseas had caught from each other, and from their taste of life in distant countries, a new sense of what it was to be a Canadian.

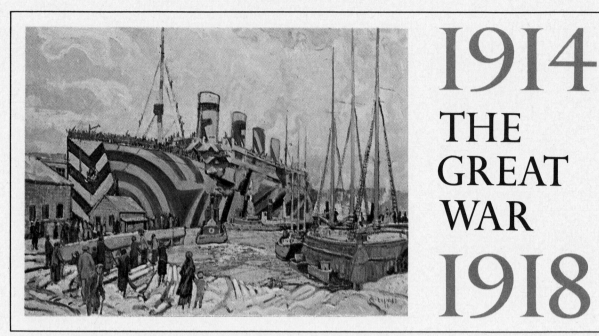

1914
THE
GREAT
WAR
1918

Arthur Lismer: Olympic with Returned Soldiers

More than four hundred thousand Canadians "proceeded over-seas," in the dusty words of the War Records Office, to make the world safe for democracy. Fifty thousand died. And in most of the places where Canadian soldiers came together, living or dead, an artist was there to paint the scene. For this was the war to end wars, and after it, clearly, should rise the monument to end monuments. So reasoned the man mainly responsible for the grand design of The Canadian War Memorials. More than a hundred artists, a score or more Canadian and the rest British, were assigned to paint Canada's war from the recruiting stations at home to the white crosses in Flanders. An architect drew blue-prints for a permanent shrine: "The Memorial, when complete, is to have more in common with the Pantheon in Paris, than with the ordinary round of fatiguing and bewildering picture galleries." The world has since played false with all the good intentions of that day. The blueprints for the Pantheon were mislaid or lost. The man whose great design the Memorial was, Sir Max Aitken, later Lord Beaverbrook, watched the dust gather on both the Memorial paintings and the British Empire, which he had expected the war to cement forever. But the paintings, at least, can be dusted off and often are: several hundred oils and drawings, kept at the National Gallery in Ottawa, of which some of the most moving appear on the following pages.

Eric Kennington: The Conquerors. *Kennington, an English painter, went with the war-hardened 16th Canadian Scottish when they marched from Arras to Amiens to relieve UK troops. Writers called them "storm troops."*

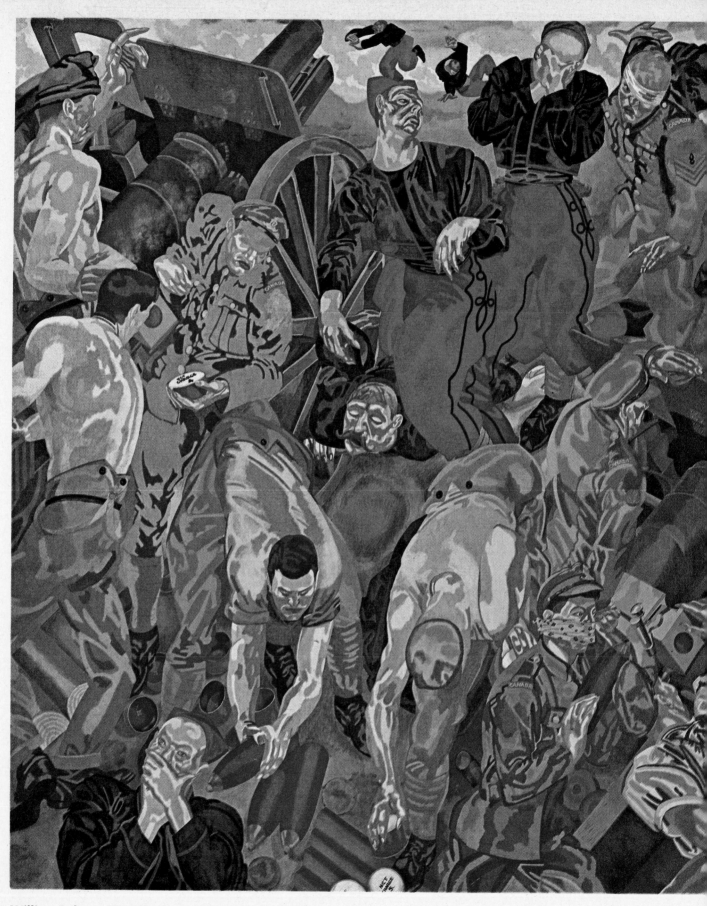

William Roberts: The First German Gas Attack at Ypres. *As the gas rolled in, French Colonial troops—mainly Zouaves and Turcos—ran. The Canadian gunners stood fast. German troops were 200 yards away.*

54

Francis H. Johnston: A Tragic Incident at Camp Borden. *Johnston, who later signed his first name "Franz" to paintings of the Canadian Shield that are now famous, was assigned to paint the air force in action. Training planes were rudimentary; tragedy was commonplace.*

A style of painting
to match the harshness of war

When William Roberts painted the gas attack at Ypres, left, he was a gunner in the British Army. He was never promoted, but he was later recognized as one of the foremost painters of a school called Vorticists. The name was coined by Ezra Pound in 1913; Wyndham Lewis made it famous. Their idea was the supremacy of machines over men; their colours were hard and bright; their perspective was flat and the action in their pictures was violent and choppy. Roberts was still painting in this style in 1965. The other Vorticists had long abandoned the style, but you can see what it taught commercial artists in almost any magazine illustration of the last thirty years.

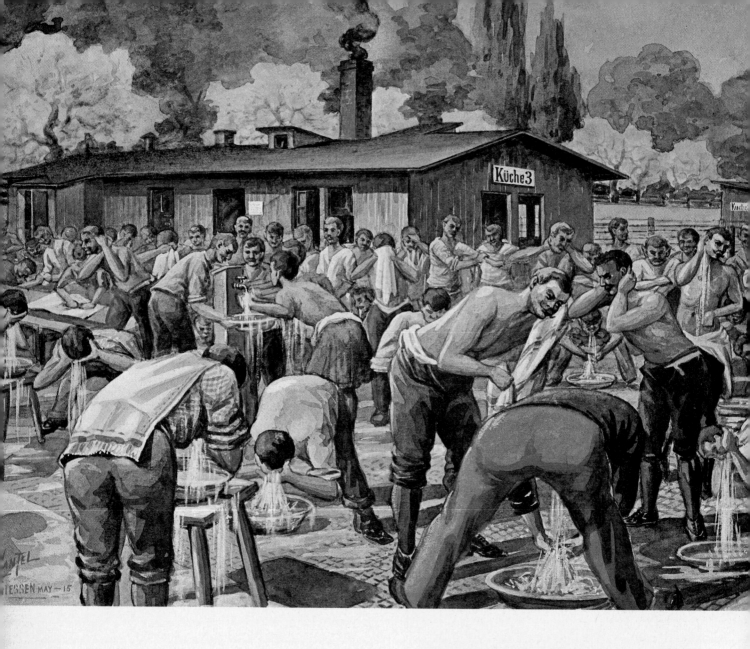

Above. Private Arthur Nantel: Every Day in the Week –
6 a.m. *Nantel was a gifted amateur, an infantryman who
was captured in the second Battle of Ypres. He made a
series of drawings he called* Sketches of Prison Life in
a German Internment Camp and War Incidents. *There
are traces of the Vorticists' style (previous page) in the
hard-edged figures and choppy motions of the men (above)
washing up outside the cookshack at Geissen prison camp.*

Ambrose McEvoy: A Portrait of Filip Konowal, V.C.
*McEvoy was an English painter commissioned a major;
Konowal was a Russian-born Canadian who enlisted in
the 43rd Battalion. Late in the war Konowal's section was
on a mopping-up job. "In one cellar," the London Gazette
reported, "he himself bayoneted three enemy, and attacked single-handed seven others . . . killing them all."
Later, he attacked and killed two machine-gun crews.*

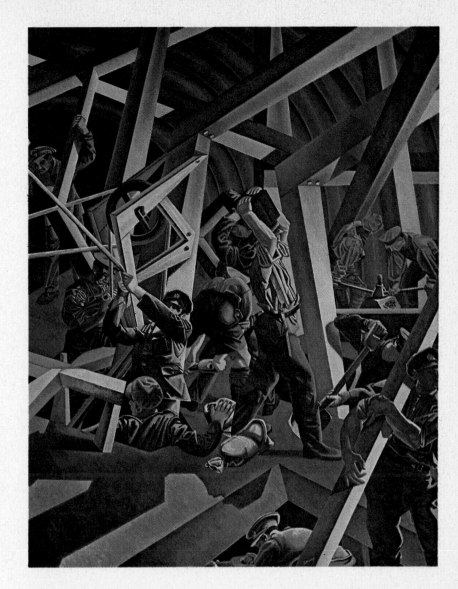

David Bomberg: Sappers at Work. *This is another painting in the Vorticist style. Bomberg, an Englishman, was assigned to Canadian Tunnelling Co. R14 at St. Eloi. Canadians did much of the heavy tunnelling for the Allies; here, R14 is hauling up sandbags filled with earth from the junction of a sap, or set of deep, zig-zag trenches.*

Louis Keene: Canadians Outside Depot in Siberia. *Between the fall of 1918 and the spring of 1919, four thousand Canadian soldiers fought a phoney war in Vladivostok. They were there to aid the White Russians against the Bolsheviks, but they never fired a shot. By April, the Canadians all had one slogan: "Home or Fight!" Home it was.*

5 HOW THE SUN SET ON BRITISH NORTH AMERICA

On April 16, 1919, the acting prime minister cabled Sir Robert Borden at the Paris Peace Conference the cabinet's alarm over the spread of bolshevism in British Columbia. He asked if Borden would get a British cruiser from the China Station to sail for Vancouver, where its presence would have "a steadying influence." Borden replied that Canada had taken care of its own rebellions since 1885, and would not change course now. Just as he had during the war, and as Laurier had before him, Borden was stubbornly holding out against British pressure to integrate Canada into the Empire. The former colony was about to become a member of the League of Nations. The idea of intimidating Canadians by means of the British navy was hardly in keeping with the new national mood.

Revolution, however, was not unthinkable. The giddy success of the Soviet workers in their ten days that shook the world had convinced an active minority of labour leaders that the sudden end of capitalism might be achieved. On every side there were pent-up hopes for a better society, born of the dislocation and sacrifices of war. There was disillusionment with the values of a world that could send ten million men marching to their death in a quagmire. The troops came back from overseas to cities alive with unrest. Workers saw their wages swallowed up by galloping inflation that seemed to benefit only the profiteer. They were ready to follow the radical leadership of the One Big Union founded at Calgary in 1919, though they were never clear about its objectives or the means to achieve them.

During the winter of 1918-19, industrial strikes were called at the rate of a dozen a month. On May 13, 1919, after employers refused to bargain collectively with two thousand metal workers striking for eighty-five cents an hour and a forty-four-hour week, the Winnipeg Trades and Labour Council decided to use the ultimate weapon. A general strike was called. Milk drivers and policemen and telegraph operators – everyone – walked off their jobs. The thirty-five thousand strikers, with their families, numbered half the population of Winnipeg. A silent paralysis descended on the city, which was governed, in effect, from Labour Temple. A few essential stores and delivery wagons kept going, but they bore the sign, "Permitted by Authority of Strike Committee."

Then a group of leading citizens improvised a counter-revolution. They set up a radio station on top of the *Free Press* building from which to communicate with the outside world. The senior staff began publishing the newspapers once more. The mayor was emboldened to speak out against the strike. Some men drifted back to work. Impatiently, the returned soldiers among the strikers broke the plan of passive resistance and began street marches. The federal government moved in on June seventeenth to arrest eight of the strike leaders. On June twenty-first the mounted city police clattered down Main Street and fought their way through a huge crowd. As they were about to be engulfed they fired three volleys into the crowd from their forty-fives, killing two and wounding many, and not long afterwards all resistance collapsed.

On doubtful evidence six of the strike leaders, including a Methodist minister and a city alderman, were sent to prison. One of those acquitted was a scholarly pacifist who had resigned his Christian ministry during the war and worked for a time on the Vancouver dock front, J. S. Woodsworth. As MP for Winnipeg North Centre from 1921 on, and later as first national leader of the CCF (now New Democratic) Party, Woodsworth was to become the voice of Canada's social conscience. Though he never formed a government, he was the Canadian whose influence probably did most in the long run to change the unjust

During the Winnipeg General Strike, workers published their own paper. Good news—as above—was rare.

Strikers, 35,000 strong, and families made up half the population of Winnipeg. They clogged the streets.

world the strikers complained of and fought against.

Woodsworth's Winnipeg was a polyglot community with a British majority, a French-Canadian enclave, and peoples from every part of Europe—it was a world centre of Ukrainian culture and had a heavier concentration of Jews for its size than any other city in North America. It was for long the rallying ground of social democracy in Canada. It was also the capital of wheat, the metropolis of the western farmer, and thanks to the strong voice of John W. Dafoe, the editor of the *Free Press*, it was the focal point of Canadian liberalism, as George Brown's Toronto had been in his day.

In January, 1920, the farm groups of Canada met in Winnipeg to found the Progressive Party, which astounded everyone by taking sixty-five seats in the federal election of 1921, fifteen more than the Conservative government. The Progressives refused to recognize that they were in fact in politics. They declined to become the official opposition even though they were the second largest group in the House. This fact, along with their distrust of the labour movement, dissipated their strength. Similarly, the political naivete and inexperience of the Farmers' governments that took office in Alberta and Ontario in 1919 eventually proved their undoing. In federal politics the strength of western agrarian radicalism was swallowed up for a time by the Liberals; later, metamorphosed in the

soul of John Diefenbaker, essentially the same protest movement seized control of what had become the Progressive Conservative Party. From 1919 on, the west has had a continuous history of distrust for the two old parties, and has furnished much of the variety and ferment of Canadian politics.

Just as in later years the prairies formed the most nationalistic audience for Canadian magazines and radio, the needs of the Protestant mission churches there gave impetus to the movement that created in 1925 the United Church of Canada, "a national organization expressing the soul of Canada,"as one clergyman described it. Since the nineteenth century the churches, both by deliberate policy and by the very fact of their national scope, had played a crucial role in helping Canadians to become aware of themselves as a nation. The new nation-wide professional organizations—of doctors and lawyers, manufacturers and scholars—along with a host of social influences, from Eaton's catalogue to the Canadian Clubs, culminated in a burst of national feeling in the Jubilee year, 1927. The political framework of 1867 had now been lived in for three generations.

A new cultural nationalism showed itself—in the founding of the Canadian Historical Association, for example, whose leading members began to rewrite their country's history as the story of the rise of nationhood. The first substantial Canadian publishing industry sprang into being during the 1920s, and brought out no fewer than six histories of Canadian literature. Canadian poets were booked for lecture tours and literary summer camps. The Canadian Authors Association founded Canada Book Week and put up posters that said: "700 Canadian Authors in our Wonderful Canada. Have you read their books?" Though the newly founded *Canadian Forum* expressed its disdain for the inane pretensions of such crude literary nationalism, it was itself a manifestation of the new national feeling.

Fine painters had flourished in Canada earlier, but members of the Group of Seven were the first to create a Canadian national style. In crude, slashing brush strokes and strong colours they celebrated the primal terror and vitality of the Laurentian Shield. Like the bush pilots and the prospectors, the arctic explorers and the Peace River wheat farmers under the high subarctic summer sun, they penetrated the solemn lands of the Canadian north and made them part of the Canadian experience.

But during these years and for a whole generation after, artists portrayed little of Canada's urban, industrial life. With the single exception of F. H. Varley, none really looked into the depths of a human face, and few for that matter suggested that Canadians had faces at all. Most Canadian fiction writers, unlike Morley Callaghan, who told of real human beings living in real cities, were content to portray the mindless gestures of stock figures from the attics of irrelevant old realisms and second-hand romance.

In politics, the new national spirit took the form of an independent Canadian foreign policy and the definition of equal status under the Crown for the self-governing dominions of the Empire. On these issues, French and English Canadians found common ground. Under the new Liberal leader, Mackenzie King, and his Quebec partner Ernest Lapointe, the nation entered upon a time of healing that saved it for many years from another racial confrontation as bitter as that of 1917.

Young Mr. King hardly looked like a man who was to spend the better part of thirty years as prime minister. "A little fat round man," as he confided to himself in Prufrockian soliloquy, with "no expression of a lofty character," he sought lonely solace singing hymns to himself, confiding in his diary and his dog, in spiritual conversation with a few select ladies, and in communion with the voice of his adored mother and family from the world beyond. Of pious, earnest,

unprepossessing public manner, he sat in the House of Commons in the uncomfortable, often terrifying presence of his lean, handsome, high-principled Conservative rival, Arthur Meighen, who stated his views with fearless clarity and used the most withering tongue in Canadian parliamentary history to pour scorn on the devious moralistic meanderings of King's mind and policies. But Meighen had two fatal flaws. He would not conciliate at the cost of being illogical, and he could not quite read, or act with, the temper of his times. He managed to appear to the public as an imperialist, as an enemy of Quebec, and as the opponent of the revolutionary postwar expectations of the common man.

King, by contrast, the theorist of social reform, labour expert, and former settlement-house worker, sought discreetly the alliance of Woodsworth and the Progressives against even his own right-wing Liberals. Conciliation of the strong new sectional interests was second nature to him. Meighen denounced him for preaching free trade on the prairies, protection in Ontario, anti-conscription in Quebec and humbug in the Maritimes. King beat him in three general elections. A ruthless politician who was convinced that the guiding hand of Providence was with him, King could use daggers, even if he spoke none, on anyone – even his own governor-general – who crossed his political path. His busy conscience, though it continually nagged, never finally passed judgment against him.

After he had put Meighen, still in his prime, out of public life in 1926, King breathed easier. Presiding over the fat prosperous years of the later 1920s, he occupied alone the dead centre of the political spectrum. He was, after all, a former adviser to the Rockefellers as well as a rebel's grandson.

During this time of never-ending bounty the high hopes and grim realities of wartime fell away in the distance. A variety of new light industries and the new products of Canada's forests and mines brought ever-increasing prosperity. The stock markets floated easily upwards to dizzying heights in the long hot summer of 1929. Normalcy and continental isolation in America seemed enough. Then the market dipped on September third and began its disastrous plunge down the long slope into the next decade. Canadians entered upon a time of troubles at home and in a world abroad that had not after all been made safe for democracy. They were rudely reminded that their society was far from the heavenly kingdom they had counted on in 1919.

THE AGE OF FLIGHT DAWNS

The bush pilot, like his lineal ancestors, the *coureur de bois* and the *voyageur*, is a unique Canadian type, spawned by the nature of the tattered terrain he patrols. In the late 1920s and early 1930s he bound the north to Canada as the railway had the west in the 1880s. Without him, the north would have remained asleep. Thus the bush pilot, in all his manifestations, is an authentic Canadian hero, the human repository of all those qualities typical Canadians are *not* supposed to have: daring, imagination, romantic courage, a sense of adventure and a gambling spirit—all those qualities, indeed, which in World War I turned raw young men from Winnipeg, Nanaimo and Owen Sound into knights of the air. It was, after all, a Canadian, Roy Brown, who shot down the great von Richthofen, thus saving the bacon of another Canadian, Wop May, who was destined to become the first great folk figure of the new air age. With the advent of that new era, Canadians became aware that their country was at last on the crossroads of the world. From Edmonton to Newfoundland, the pace setters and record breakers roared across the oceans, around the globe and over the pole. And far off in the lake-flecked hinterland, small brown children, who had never seen a streetcar or a Model A Ford, had already learned to spot a Fokker, Junkers or Norseman at ten miles.

In 1911, J. A. D. McCurdy, Canada's pioneer aviator, tried the first U.S.-Cuba flight over shark-infested waters. His oil pressure failed a mile from the coast and he lost the $10,000 prize.

Pioneers and pacemakers

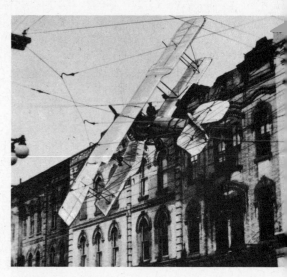

Early airship of Japanese silk, varnished with raw linseed oil and driven by a motorcycle engine, was piloted at Montreal air meet of 1910 by 17-year-old Cromwell Dixon. Ship crashed just after this picture was made. Dixon was killed in 1911.

Famous Curtiss Jenny wartime trainer, had top speed of 75 m.p.h. It could smash into Oshawa telephone wires without killing the pilot Barnstormers loved it.

Fred McCall, Canada's sixth-ranking air ace, saved lives at Calgary Exhibition in 1919 by choosing to crash-land his stalled Jenny on very centre of a rotating merry-go-round.

Wing walkers of the early 1920s became the bush pilots of the next decade. For stunts they preferred the Jenny biplane.

In 1919, John Alcock (left) and Arthur Brown (right) took off from Newfoundland on the first successful trans-Atlantic flight.

In 1930, Charles Kingsford-Smith, first man across the Pacific, manoeuvred his famous Southern Cross through the fog and into Harbour Grace en route from Ireland to New York.

In 1931, on first day of record aerial dash around the world, Wiley Post and Harold Gatty landed Winnie Mae at Newfoundland. Eight days later: Edmonton.

An earlier attempt to circle the world by John Mears and Henry Brown had ended in disaster on precisely the same spot. Their Lockheed Vega went out of control just before lift-off and was a total wreck. Both pilots escaped injury.

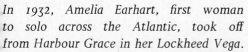

In 1932, Amelia Earhart, first woman to solo across the Atlantic, took off from Harbour Grace in her Lockheed Vega.

In 1936, Robert Merrill, with nightclub singer Harry Richman, set a new trans-Atlantic speed record of 210 m.p.h. Public's fancy was caught by wings full of ping pong balls.

War ace Wop May became famous bush pilot, flew first mail to Arctic.

Stranded in arctic weather for almost a year, this plane when finally refuelled flew perfectly, as its makers boasted.

U.S.-born Katherine Stinson, twenty-two, flew the first airmail on prairies.

1919: Two V.C.s, W. A. Barker (left) and "Billy" Bishop, tried out passenger service between Toronto and Muskoka. It flopped.

This durable Vickers Viking amphibian, many times dismantled, flew on three coasts and in almost every province before fire destroyed it in 1932. Its equally durable pilot, Jack Caldwell (foreground), became, in 1929, the first Canadian to save his own life by parachute.

War aces
become
bush pilots
as the mail
goes
through

*First trans-Canada flight in 1920 was made in hops by a ser-
ies of aircraft-and-pilot teams. Shown arriving in Calgary
from Regina: Capt. A. E. Cudmore and Lt.-Col. Arthur Tylee.*

*Tylee and fresh pilot, Capt. G. A. Thompson, took off in second
DH-9a (shipped from Eastern Canada) on final lap of journey.
This was the first aerial crossing of the Selkirk mountains.*

6 THE SCARS OF A DISHONEST DECADE

Things happened in the 1930s by radio. And so they happened more intensely, more privately, all at once, to everyone, with the clarity of a dream or a nightmare. People plunged deep into the sound – of the Louis-Schmeling fights and the marathon swims at the CNE, of swing and soap opera, of the sagacity of a pair of chuckleheads named Amos 'n' Andy and of a monocled wooden dummy in a top hat named Charlie McCarthy, who was cynical and at the same time innocent, the way a boy had to be to outface the meanness and terror of the times. Even the commercials played on the nerves of self-doubt and uncertainty: the foghorn blowing B.O. seemed somehow more real than the hopeful harbour bell singing "Lifebuoy."

The biggest sound from coast to coast came from the roaring echo-chamber of a sports palace, and a voice glistening as ice and sharp as a skate vibrated with the heroic action of Hockey Night in Canada. There were sometimes broadcasts, too, of another frenzied crowd in another sports palace, louder and more rhythmic, and another screaming, hypnotic voice, this one politely interspersed with "Herr Hitler has just said . . ." in the accent of Stanley Baldwin's England. The meaning of that sound was too terrible to reflect on, except as something from a different planet: and sure enough the winged horror lit and walked the streets of the continent one Sunday evening in 1938. The fantasy of Orson Welles's invasion from Mars told the radio audience again what they knew in their bones, that the war of the world was coming, in some places had already come.

But there were troubles that walked by day, and closer to home. At first, in the 1929 crash, it was mainly the foolish rich who suffered. The solidest of the Canadian bankers and industrialists were protected by the caution they had exercised during the boom.

It was what followed the crash, year in and year out, that hurt everyone. The great depression settled its deadly blight upon the land. It was a time of helplessness in the face of some terrible, grim, nameless inertia, a time for the acceptance of silent indignity. Of its causes there seemed to be no understanding, and for its curing no remedy. Home for many people became linked with the idea of eviction or with living in basements or garages or tarpaper shanty towns, or watching while the threat crept up on others, and nothing able to stop it.

The great transcontinental railways, which had been the symbol and the means of the Dominion's prosperity and its very existence, now dragged the mockery of themselves and the hope they had offered – empty box-cars bearing uninvited passengers, moving back and forth endlessly across the nation in search of work or a handout. At first an effort was made by the railways to keep the men off, but they soon gave up trying.

In the steel towns of Sydney and Hamilton and the Sault, open hearths and blast furnaces stood idle for months on end. There was a three-month spell in the spring of 1933 when no pig-iron was made at all in Canada, for the first time since the eighteenth century.

The price of prairie wheat dropped to the lowest recorded level in history, thirty-eight cents a bushel. The income of Saskatchewan declined to a quarter of what it had been. And over the dry lands, like a prophecy, came the drought. The black blizzards blew off the topsoil, leaving sand dunes where once wheat had grown forty bushels to the acre. Society reverted to barter. In some places doctors and teachers were paid in vegetables or cords of wood if they were paid at all. In the rural Maritimes and Quebec, people were used to poverty; for many there was little they had not faced before. It was harder in the great cities. Young

Foster Hewitt in the 1920s: "radio's biggest sound."

Tim Buck at Maple Leaf Gardens: 17,000 cheered him.

men who were one day destined to run the largest enterprises in Canada tramped the city streets trying to pick up half-dollars doing odd jobs. Sometimes a householder would give away a dime, like old John D. Rockefeller (still confident and alert in his nineties with an income larger than those of most Canadian provinces). A dime would get the man a bowl of soup and coffee at Bowles Lunch, though John D's advice, like that of all his kind, was not to squander the dime but to save it. Sir Herbert Holt, the only Canadian in history who ever had anything remotely like the corporate power of a Rockefeller, was a recluse and gave no dimes away, but he was enough of a legend in his time for the crowd to gasp, then cheer, when his death was announced over the loudspeaker at Delorimier Stadium in Montreal.

The army thought of a plan for the vagrant unemployed. Put them in work camps; give them something to do and a bit of discipline. Hoping to avoid potential riots or something worse, the government found it had only hived men up for the organizers. By the spring of 1935 the western work campers were ready to march on Ottawa. On June third a thousand men boarded the CPR's night freight out of Vancouver.

Their numbers grew as the train moved across Alberta, and there were a thousand more waiting at Winnipeg. Alarmed, the government persuaded the marchers to get off at Regina with a guarantee of meal tickets and an offer to meet their leaders. Here the authorities began a war of attrition against the marchers. The townspeople were forbidden to give them food or money. In defiance, their leaders called a mass meeting for the evening of Dominion Day in Market Square. A children's bicycle brigade ferried rocks into the square for the marchers. Then four moving-vans full of constables with baseball bats and a squad of armed city police drove in. When the fighting was over, downtown Regina was a shambles, one city detective was dead, several dozen men had gunshot wounds, and a hundred were in jail. The great unjailed majority left their encampment at the Regina Exhibition grounds next day, filing past mounted sub-machine guns, and scattered back across the west they had come from. All the work camps were disbanded. You couldn't go home again, even to that.

Tim Buck, just out of Kingston Penitentiary and hero for a day, spoke to seventeen thousand people packed into Maple Leaf Gardens and had a boulevard

Houde and Duplessis: smiling strongmen ran Quebec.

R. B. Bennett was "loud, ebullient, but not a leader."

in Alberta named after him. But the spirit of Lenin, the greatest history-maker of the twentieth century, was vastly more important to Canada than any number of Tim Bucks. So was fascism. So too was the American recovery under F.D.R. These were the great forces that were shaping the world, and the times were doubly frustrating for a Canadian because his nation could do so little to affect them. If you wanted to act in those days, and not merely to be acted upon by the great events and ideas, you had to go where they were happening. To claim his birthright as a compatriot of Mackenzie and Papineau a Canadian had to leave, as Dr. Norman Bethune did, for Spain or China.

French Canada met the depression, as it had met so many threats to its existence before, by a strategy of survival. The French withdrew into memory, and sought a chief, the last and the biggest chief of all, who by his power and charm kept the natives in order and took his toll of favours from the American corporations and the English-speaking barons of St. James Street and the Montreal *Gazette*. The election of

68

Maurice Duplessis in 1936 meant that another generation would pass before the French-Canadian nation would enter fully into its heritage of political maturity and the twentieth century.

The rest of Canada became more American. Unlike the transcontinental railways running east and west, the new roads went south. The cars themselves were styled in America. So were George Gershwin's songs and Shirley Temple's movies, Bruno Hauptmann and Jean Harlow and Fiorello La Guardia, Monopoly and Big Little Books, the FBI, the CIO and *Gone With The Wind*. They all became part of our culture. There were no new songs or myths about Canadian things and places. Even when the local product was popular it had an American model: Major Bowes' Amateur Hour for Ken Soble, Hoover Wagons for Bennett Buggies. Canada's favourite gangster, Red Ryan, met life and death Chicago style, and Benny Goodman, really, not Bert Niosi, was Canada's king of swing. When Canadians made good, it was usually, like Walter Pidgeon or Deanna Durbin, as Americans, unless of course they

Followers of William Aberhart, Alberta's first Social Credit premier, called him Honest Abe.

were the Dionne quintuplets, who made as much copy for the Hearst press as the rest of the Canadian stories of the decade combined.

Another exception was The Monarchy, more intimately part of English-Canadian culture than at any time before or since. The three-cent carmine jubilee stamps of George V and Mary were still being soaked from the envelopes when the school principal announced at assembly that the dying King had asked his subject children to sing the anthem this morning as a prayer, and awe-struck, they did. There were no stamps for the new King, but he was more interesting. When she was told that the King was going to marry Mrs. Simpson, the dear old lady in Nut Mountain, Saskatchewan, asked, "What will Lady Eaton do now?" And when Edward renounced his throne for the woman he loved some Canadians were not clear whether they disliked her more because she was divorced or because she was American. Radio brought the Empire into all the Christmas living rooms. George VI may have been the only genuinely loved

monarch in Canadian history. Families sat anxious and sympathetic on their sofa edges as the spasmic, good man wrestled and gagged out the platitudes that somehow turned true in the travail of the uttering; they stood solemnly embarrassed facing the radio while the band played at the end. Then the Royal Couple came. They waved and smiled. The Royal Train rolled three thousand miles across their silver effigies, placed under its wheels in tribute and sacrifice. And Canadians were readier than they had been to fight and pray for the King who would lead them into war.

There was no statesman to lead Canada into battle against the depression. Instead of the fireside manner and brave facing of facts, Canadians were given a choice between two rather settled, well-fed bachelors – Bennett, the loud, ebullient one who barked and blasted at the depression in the name of sound money and self-help, of high tariffs and a happier bygone age; and King, the prim, careful, quiet one who befogged the issues and choices ("Not a New Deal, but a Square Deal") until the war came and blew the depression

John W. Dafoe, almost alone, warned against Fascism.

away and Canada recovered its nerve and a sense of purpose. William Aberhart, the one completely successful politician of the 1930s, was a sort of WASP Father Divine, didactic and respectable and surprisingly in touch with his age, who took and held a whole province captive by means of radio, the Bible, and a pat formula for making money help people instead of hurting them.

Social Credit was to politics what chiropractic was to medicine and the evangelical sects were to the established churches. It had a simple answer for trouble, and it appealed warmly and deeply to people for whom conventional society and methods offered little hope or made little sense. It was built on a province-wide organization of cells that gathered to discuss the weekly radio messages of William Aberhart. When Aberhart discovered the arithmetic of Social Credit he added it to his gospel and moved into politics in 1935 without missing a step. In his vest and rimless glasses, bald, benign but stern, like everybody's old-fashioned high school principal, Aberhart breathed an air of certainty and the power of positive thinking. He was a combination of William Jennings Bryan, Frank

Buchman and Mr. Micawber. His adoring followers called him Honest Abe and compared him to F.D.R., despite his modest disclaimer ("a much greater reformer than I"). There was a tinge of British Israelitism about him—for Aberhart it was the King James Version of the Bible that was the literal word of God. Though Social Credit was too pragmatic and eclectic really to be regarded as another of those semi-fascist movements that blew through the western democracies in the 1930s, it was nevertheless a party of the right, committed to free enterprise while at the same time offering fascism's hope of radical change. It was to remain in power in Alberta for over thirty years, and after adapting with ease to prosperity and spreading to the other western empire province in the person of another formidable character, W.A.C. "Wacky" Bennett of British Columbia, it almost looked as though it could hold on in the west for the rest of the twentieth century.

Social Credit had its right-wing counterpart in Ontario in Premier Mitchell Hepburn, the raucous, brawling young onion farmer whose platform manner —and use of the police against the newly organized CIO—invited comparison with Huey Long. And in Quebec Maurice Duplessis talked and acted almost as though he believed in the ideals of Mussolini and his corporate state.

Continental isolation was the essence of Canada's foreign policy during the years when Japan was building her Greater East Asia Co-prosperity Sphere and Hitler was threatening the peace of Europe. Mackenzie King undoubtedly reflected the mood of the Canadian people when he disowned his delegate's resolution at the League of Nations to cut off the oil supplies for Mussolini's invasion of Ethiopia. That was the League's last hope for effective action. When King called on Hitler after attending the 1937 Coronation, he found the führer a simple man too unintelligent to be dangerous. After Munich, King cabled Chamberlain that the heart of Canada was rejoicing. The Toronto *Star* gave more play to the Moose River mine disaster and rescue than to all the foreign stories of the year. So it continued right up to the day before Hitler invaded Poland. Almost alone, Dafoe of the *Free Press* reprinted Churchill's warnings against the fascist powers, and accused King of politely ushering the League of Nations into outer darkness. But with troubles enough to occupy them at home, Canadians, as someone later said, were content to send their sympathy to the beleaguered Chinese and their scrap metal to Japan.

MACKENZIE KING

the unknown Canadian

His life was an eerie alternation of limelight and shadow. At the University of Toronto in the 1890s (left) he was in everybody's eye as a "campus orator, agitator and social climber." He was also a prig, a man more at home with himself than other people. As prime minister (right, campaigning in 1926) he was a busy but unnatural host. He felt "a real sense of rest and freedom in being again alone with Pat (his Irish terrier)," he wrote after a guest left Laurier House. In truth, he was often alone with specters; he was a mystic who began by sensing the hand of God on his shoulder – "I feel I am being guided from above" – and ended by taking counsel from the dead at professional seances. He guarded his secret well. Although he penetrated the nation's entire life, as Bruce Hutchison wrote, the nation could never penetrate the life of its leader.

The Family Album of a future Prime Minister

Alive, and beyond the grave, King's family remained the most important people in his life. At first his lawyer father was able to maintain a "comfortable, genteel" home, in which his mother dominated his upbringing and personality. Later, sickness and bad luck made them dependent on King; supporting them he developed an almost miserly respect for money.

At two: his doting Mother, who called him "Billy," primped the child and schooled him in her ambition.

At twenty-two: he went from school into the slums as a social worker, a zealous but callow reformer.

*Ottawa man: in 1905,
already a confidante of Laurier,
he went west looking
like a typical eastern dude.*

*Travelling man: within
days, he was dressing like an
Albertan and posing with
chiefs on a foothills reserve.*

*Family man: he tried to
make his only close friend,
W. A. Harper, one of the circle.
His mother and sister Jenny
(on the grass) were delighted.*

The Ladies in his Life

In his late thirties, out of office and almost out of money, Mackenzie King set out on his longest, most arduous losing campaign. The object was to find a wife: "To go into politics without marrying wd. be folly," he wrote. "I cannot live that cruel life without a home & someone to love and be loved by . . . Marry I must." He had prospects, a ready smile brightened by a perfect set of false teeth, and many of the appropriate graces – he sometimes took himself to task for dancing too often until two in the morning. He also had one supremely important woman in his life already. This was his mother; he gave her his whole devotion, as a biographer wrote, and in return "she loved and preyed on him." When King fell genuinely in love with a nurse, his mother dissuaded him from making the poor match. When he courted women of adequate position and income, they may have felt they could afford to demand more of him than his mother was prepared to give. They all said no. He had very few real successes with women, and none involved romance. He found a woman to finance him, a woman to act as his hostess, and several women to act as his bridge between the world of the living and the worlds of the dead.

Violet Markham: she was English, older than King, and sympathetic. She was also rich; for some years, he lived on an allowance she gave to him of 300 pounds a year.

Beatrix Robb: he wrote her often; she signed this photo, "To Rex, with best wishes, Beatrix, 1928."

Mrs. Wreidt: he invited her to Kingsmere, where she staged seances – one of several mediums he trusted.

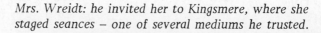

Julia Grant: he continued to write her, too, long after she had been married – to a Prince Cantacuzene.

Mrs. Patteson: he made her his formal hostess and confidential friend, but never a romantic partner.

In Colorado: he visited his brother Max, who was dying of TB. King paid the medical bills.

The public figure

King was a public figure most of his adult life. Although he was forty-seven when he first became prime minister in 1921, he had been a deputy minister (of labour) even before he was first elected to the House in 1908. At his death, in 1950, he was celebrated far beyond Canada as the leader who had remained in office longer than any other in the history of the English-speaking peoples. By this time he was also a rich man; his estate was valued at a little less than a million dollars. He had a taste for privacy, and a recurrent weight problem. (It once went well above two hundred pounds: "I do not like my appearance anywhere," he wrote. "A little fat round man . . ."). To indulge the taste and cope with the problem, he often travelled – anonymously. At these times his appearance was in contrast to the figure he cut on the public platform. At the Imperial Conference of 1926, a British trade journal picked him out as a "model of sartorial deportment."

In Ottawa: he posed for a formal portrait in formal dress. He wanted to look the leader.

becomes the anonymous tourist

Beside the sea: he swam (here, in California) for his waistline's sake.

On the sea: he cruised (here, aboard the Conte di Sonia*) for relaxation.*

7 TOTAL WAR AND THE HOME FRONT

It was going to be a short war, and France and Britain would win it by themselves. The armies massed behind the impenetrable safety of the Maginot Line. The picture weeklies displayed the laurel-wreathed *gloire* of General Gamelin's hat and the comforting understatement of Mr. Chamberlain's umbrella. The first Canadian troops arrived in Britain in December, 1939, and there was some doubt whether they were either welcome or necessary. A delegation of Canadian industrialists went over to ask the British government how Canada might contribute to the war effort, but they were politely told that British industry could take care of all present needs.

Then the blitzkrieg struck in the spring of 1940, and everything changed. For France it was indeed a short war. On the twenty-first of June Adolf Hitler entered the old Armistice railway car at Compiègne and received what amounted to the surrender of continental Europe, or what was left of it.

From that day forward, Canada was no longer merely a marginal source of moral support and a training ground for Commonwealth airmen. She was until 1941 the second largest power in the struggle against Hitler's Europe. She was called upon to throw whatever resources she could muster into the balance against the might of the most heavily industrialized area in the world.

Before the war ended one million men and women joined the Canadian armed forces. Canadian soldiers saw action on two major fronts, and her airmen fought in the skies above Britain and Europe for six years. But perhaps Canada's most crucial contribution was made at home in the total mobilization of all her resources, just as her most crucial battle, the one on which everything else depended, was fought in the North Atlantic from the Irish Sea to the Maritime ports of Canada and the Gulf of St. Lawrence.

"The Atlantic convoy was the heartbeat of the war," as the convoy's historian, Joseph Schull, wrote. "The battle could be fought, ironically enough, with the small ships, the old ships—always provided there were enough of them." By the war's end the Royal Canadian Navy had taken over four-fifths of the escort work in the North Atlantic. Although the navy was heavily involved in the Mediterranean and in the Normandy invasion, this endless herding of the flow of merchantmen, month in and month out, over the howling grey seas to Britain, was always its principal task. As Admiral Mahan said of the navy that defied Napoleon's continent: "Those far distant storm-beaten ships, upon which the Grand Army never looked, stood between it and the dominion of the world."

There were grim months on end when the loss of merchant ships far exceeded the rate of replacement. Many sailors had several ships torpedoed under them. To replace them, Canadian shipyards launched during the war nearly eight thousand small craft and well over a thousand naval and cargo vessels. Canadian industry produced in all some ten billion dollars worth of munitions and war equipment, including fifty thousand tanks and gun carriers, sixteen thousand aircraft, and most of the military transport used in the Eighth Army's drive across North Africa against Rommel. Other war costs amounted to another ten billion dollars, and beyond that, Canada gave away during the course of the war some four billion dollars worth of military aid to her allies.

Set against American war production, these amounts do not bulk large. But the Canadian contribution began early and made a crucial difference to the winning of the war. For a nation of twelve million people it was a prodigious accomplishment.

It required the utmost precision, efficiency and self-discipline in planning the whole Canadian economy. It demanded redirection of all the nation's resources and manpower by price control, by rationing and by quota systems. The task was supervised by men who, with Roosevelt's brain trust or Elizabeth I's privy councillors, could easily be ranked among the finest group of public servants in Western history; men of the calibre of Clifford Clark, Graham Towers and Donald Gordon. Working with them were many of the ablest members of the business and university communities in Canada. Leading them all, the director of the entire economy, was Clarence Decatur Howe, once described by Lord Beaverbrook, whose own war-production record earned him the right to judge, as "one of the handful of men of whom it can be said, 'But for him the war would have been lost.'"

As a young Yankee civil engineer, Howe had come north to teach at Dalhousie University and to build into the landscape of Canada the bridges and dams and the great lakehead grain elevators put up by his engineering firm. He was an intelligent, immensely generous man, formidably intolerant of opposition, with a strong, finely chiselled face that had a great reserve of power in it, ready to burst into laughter or scorn at the incompetence of fools and the devious ways of politicians. One of Howe's many legacies was the training of a whole generation of postwar leaders in business and public service. He was quite prepared to put the government into business itself, through the familiar Canadian device of the crown corporation. He and his predecessors had already established a government-owned broadcasting network and a transcontinental airline. During the war Howe created no fewer than twenty-eight new crown corporations. They ranged in scope from Eldorado Mining, which made the uranium for the atomic bomb, to Polymer, which made synthetic rubber to replace supplies cut off by the Japanese conquest of Malaya. They went a long

C. D. Howe, "director of Canada's entire economy" in World War II, organized 28 new crown corporations.

way to prove Howe's boast that never again would there be any doubt that Canada could manufacture anything that could be made elsewhere.

After the terrible years of the depression, the sudden, desperate need for everyone to work and the discovery that Canadians could do things they had not dreamed they had in them (this time without the inflation and profiteering and confusion that had occurred in 1914-18) brought on an exhilarating recovery of confidence. Yet there was no delight in war for its own sake. There was far less of that blasphemous equation of the cause of God with that of country so characteristic of World War I. There was not the appalling immobility and hopelessness of the Great War's years in the trenches. The treatment of Japanese Canadians who were forcibly moved from the west coast was possibly the blackest mark on Canada's war record. The idolizing of England marked by things like the host of Canadian OBEs and that incredible national war song, the battle hymn of the Dominion, *There'll Always Be an England*, probably

Corpses littered the beach at Dieppe in 1942. It was an inspiring – and tragic – hour for Canada.

THE EVENING TELEGRAM HOME AND SPORTS

VOL. LXIX., NO. 12   30 PAGES   TORONTO. TUESDAY. JUNE 6. 1944   PRICE THREE CENTS

ALLIES 7 MILES IN FRANCE
WIN BEACH IN 15 MINUTES

D-Day: the assault on Europe began, the Telegram reported, at 12:01 Toronto time, June 6, '44.

delayed English Canada's coming of age by a few years, but it did little real harm. Admiration for Churchill and his countrymen during the Battle of Britain, in fact, was one of the chief means by which English Canadians recovered their idealism and emerged from the craven and self-satisfied isolation of the prewar years into an appreciation of the idea of one world and their own international responsibilities.

To Mackenzie King, the prime minister who had picked Howe and Ralston and Ilsley and Power, must go the first credit for leadership of the country during the war, a fact which Canadians did not readily accept. They thought better of themselves than to be led by this strange little man, with his windy whistling academic speeches, who "never did anything by halves that he could do by quarters;" this compromising politician of the extreme centre, who always seemed to occupy the ground that belonged by right to noble,

strong, outspoken men; this frustrating price of being Canadian.

His countrymen would have been even more uncomfortable had they known that when King flew to England he did more than consult Churchill, get booed by the troops, and act as a sort of overseas uncle to the royal family. He also visited his favourite medium, and crammed his luggage with ruins from the bombed House of Commons for his strange collection of monuments at Kingsmere.

Yet without King, the "Destroyers for Bases" deal that helped save Britain would probably have failed to materialize. He was regarded with affection and respect by F.D.R., who confided to King secrets he would not tell his cabinet. This friendship, in fact, made easier and more immediately fruitful that revolutionary alignment of Canada within the North American system of defence, foreign policy and economy

80

Cheers for Churchill and King at Quebec Conference.

which was to be a central fact of her future in the twentieth century.

King was more readily given credit for a different achievement. He prevented a re-opening of the deep rift between English and French over conscription, though his action was bitterly resented by some English Canadians who felt he should have imposed conscription on the shirking and craven French. (This is a racial theory that is contradicted by the record of French-Canadian regiments during the war, the first to fill up with volunteers in 1939.) Isolationist sentiment did exist in Quebec, however. When Premier Duplessis threw down his thinly disguised threat to take Quebec out of active participation in the war, the federal Liberals, armed with King's pledge against conscription, moved into Quebec and after a hard fight beat him. Mayor Houde of Montreal was interned for urging citizens not to participate in the national registration program instituted by the federal cabinet in 1940.

Other serious criticisms of King's conduct of the war came from Premier Hepburn of Ontario, whose attacks King made the pretext for calling a federal election in 1940, and from his old rival Arthur Meighen, summoned back to politics to save the country from King. King defeated Meighen again, this time by standing aside and letting the left fight him. King humiliated three other Conservative national leaders – Bennett, Manion, and Bracken – during his career. He did it without ever having any strong personal support in the country. It was simply that he was the leader whom the largest number of Canadians could agree to tolerate, and the one who could best read their minds and emotions. He was, as the historian Frank Underhill called him, "the representative, the essential, the typical Canadian, the Canadian as he exists in the mind of God. Disliking parliament and the representative side of democracy, he worked out a much more direct relationship between himself and the people. Without any of the apparatus of mass hypnosis and police coercion to which vulgar practitioners of the art like Hitler and Mussolini had to have recourse, he succeeded with hardly a mistake in giving expression to what lay in the Canadian unconscious mind."

The most serious challenge to King's rule came at the end of the war. A generation earlier, the last wartime government in Canada had been humiliated in the first peacetime election. Churchill's government was defeated in 1945. But King read the signs of the time. In September, 1943, the polls reported that the CCF apparently had a lead of one percent in public preference over both the Liberals and Conservatives. The CCF came into power in Saskatchewan in 1944, Canada's first socialist government, and narrowly missed gaining office in the Ontario election of 1943. So in 1945 King went to the country with a program of social reform and the promise of a welfare state. Just as he had absorbed the Progressives a quarter-century before, he now took enough support away from the CCF to win power once again.

For good or ill, King's spirit haunted postwar Canada long after his death in 1950. His two successors as Liberal prime minister were both men he had chosen, and, like King himself back in Laurier's time, were originally brought into the cabinet from outside the realm of politics. Even John Diefenbaker, whom he had once bested in the riding of Prince Albert, was a disciple of King's, though one who learned more from the master in the practice of mystic communion with the popular will than he did in the art of government.

81

LAMPOONING THE USA

The heyday of political cartooning in Canada came around the turn of the century, when satiric magazines like *Grip* and *The Moon* were flourishing, mainly on the interest generated by their cartoonists' acid portraits of the politicians of the day. Men like J. W. Bengough, the cartoonist who founded *Grip*, and his leading competitor, C. W. Jefferys, were more celebrated than painters of the Academy. Later, between the World Wars, political cartooning like almost everything else went into decline – the cartoons of the time offer bland comments in a childish style. The revival came at the end of the 1950s, when the newspapers began recruiting men like Ed McNally and Duncan Macpherson, already first-rank illustrators before they turned to cartooning. In 1867 or 1967 the cartoonists' raw materials were much the same: scandal, arrogance or stupidity in high places. But of all targets, the one they have always loved best is Uncle Sam – as these pages testify.

This is how Sir John A. and Uncle Sam looked to F. J. Willson, a Canadian Illustrated News *cartoonist, in 1881.*

In 1902 The Moon *ran a cover series on* The American Girl *by A. S. Racey. Here, No. 6: Minnie-ha-ha, The Original A.G.*

The most accomplished artist of them all signed himself only "Chic." This is one of a series called Pipe Dreams.

Will Miss Canada marry Uncle Sam? "Never!" –
according to this 1886 cartoon, signed only "E.N."

GOODS PROHIBITED, BUT *EVILS* ADMITTED.

This is how J. W. Bengough saw U.S. influence in
the '80s. For similar views, see today's papers.

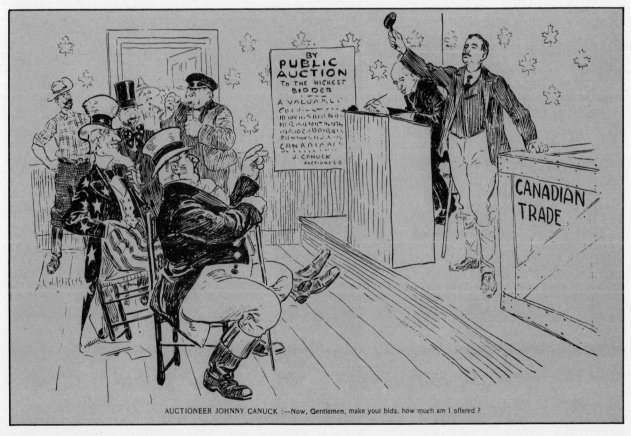

AUCTIONEER JOHNNY CANUCK :—Now, Gentlemen, make your bids, how much am I offered ?

The Great Canadian Sellout was underway in 1903,
as C. W. Jefferys saw it. But we had two bidders.

Ed McNally in the Montreal Star: *American foreign policy in the 1960s has been attacked by most cartoonists.*

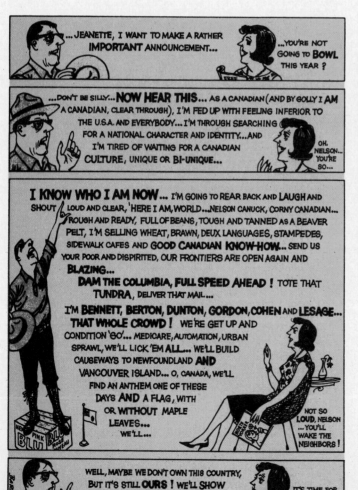

"Now to find some Canadian soil on which to plant it . . ."

Robert LaPalme in The Financial Times: *this is the problem of American ownership as one man understands it.*

Left—*Sid Barron in Maclean's: the "search for Canadian identity" has its lighter side, as Barron shows.*

" . . . O Canada, we stand on guard for thee . . . O Canada . . . "

Len Norris in the Vancouver Sun: *usually a gentle sa-*
tirist, Norris turned tough during the Bomarc dispute.

Below — *Duncan Macpherson in the Toronto Star: here,*
by an artist some call a genius, is where we stand today.

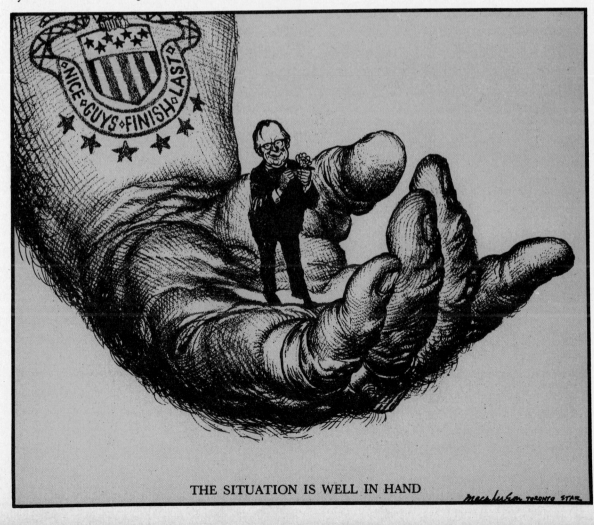

THE SITUATION IS WELL IN HAND

1945

1967

8 A NEW CANADA IN A CHANGED WORLD

Before the war a Liberal senator had spoken of Canada as "a fireproof house" in her North American isolation, and Mackenzie King had lectured the Europeans in the League of Nations about the need to use "reason" instead of "force." But in the postwar world, under a French-Canadian foreign minister, Louis St. Laurent, and a brilliant diplomatic corps led by Lester Pearson, Canadian foreign policy took an entirely new direction. Canada became one of the leading supporters of the United Nations and chief architect of the UN's role as commander of a small international police force. Canadian soldiers and diplomats were involved in peacekeeping operations in every part of the world, from the jungles of Vietnam and the Congo to the Negev desert and the mountains of Cyprus. This role was rarely glamorous or stirring; it was usually inconclusive and often quite possibly ineffective. Canadians, however, like many of the people of the newer nations, looked to the UN and the spirit of its Declaration of Human Rights not as a panacea but rather in the spirit of Winston Churchill's remark about democracy: it was the worst system in the world, except for the others.

The North Atlantic Treaty Organization involved the first appearance of Canadian forces in Europe during peacetime. The idea of NATO had been worked out by Canadians as much as anyone. It was a new but rather familiar version of what one historian called the North Atlantic Triangle, that state of tension and balance between the two larger powers of Britain and the United States in relation to Canada which had so long been the central fact of Canadian history.

Canada also had a new role to play in Asia, not only as part of the UN action in Korea, and as a member of the Colombo Plan, but in many smaller ways made possible by her middle-power status and her lack of an imperial past. She refused to join SEATO, however, preferring to maintain the confidence of Nehru's India by resisting the temptation to catch military "pactomania," as one Canadian scholar called it at the time. Canada's special relationship with India was not always fondly appreciated in the Washington of John Foster Dulles, as the nickname "Swami" Pearson indicated, but the relationship was accepted and used.

The climax of Canada's role as a conciliator in the postwar world came in the Suez crisis of 1956. The reckless adventure of Israel, France and Britain in invading Egypt at the end of October, 1956, brought on one of the great crises of the twentieth century, and the only one in which a Canadian has played a major part in making the peace. Rarely had there been an outbreak of so many-sided a trial of strengths and such a variety of hostile feelings. At Suez the aspirations of new nationalisms and ancient traditions, the memories of an imperial lifeline and of former colonial policies, the bitter Middle Eastern struggle between Arab and Jew, and the confrontation at the brink between the Soviet Union and the Western Alliance were all stirred up together. On October thirtieth, after the government of Egypt declined to obey a British ultimatum to withdraw troops from a portion of Egyptian territory on twelve hours notice, the Royal Air Force bombed Egyptian airfields. Five days later British troops landed in Port Said as if nothing had changed since the days of the Khedive and Lord Cromer. About a thousand Egyptian soldiers and civilians were killed. The Soviet Union threatened to rain rockets on London and Paris. The Americans, at the climax of a presidential election campaign, were determined to push through a flat condemnation of the invasion of Egypt, placing their country for once beside the neutralist nations at the UN. The Western Alliance was on the verge of dissolution, and if it could

Quebec, 1945: L. B. Pearson at first meeting of FAO.   *When Canada kept the peace: the Suez crisis of '56.*

be deemed to matter at such a time, so was the Commonwealth.

In hindsight, it is easy to see the United Nations Emergency Force to which Canada contributed the commander, General E. L. M. Burns, and the largest number of troops, as a simple and obvious solution to the problem. But it met at first the solidly based scepticism of even the secretary-general, Dag Hammarskjold himself. The Canadian motion proposing it, for which Canadians mounted a round-the-clock campaign to elicit delegates' support, eventually made

it possible for all the powers involved to withdraw from the extreme courses to which they were committed. Canada and, what mattered, the UN emerged from the week still holding the confidence or acceptance of all parties concerned, of Washington and Cairo and London as well as the uncommitted nations, and without at least the overt hostility of Moscow, Paris and Tel Aviv.

Pearson returned home to be denounced by the Conservative opposition in the House for his softness towards the cowardly bully, Nasser, for his failure to

89

respond to the Mother Country in her hour of need, and for being the choreboy of the United States. He replied that his government's record over the past ten years gave them the right to say that they had performed no such role. "It is bad to be a choreboy of the United States. It is equally bad to be a colonial choreboy running around shouting, 'Ready, aye, ready.' "

Three years later, when another crisis in Commonwealth relations arose, a Conservative prime minister was to go further than the Liberals had earlier thought feasible. John Diefenbaker sided with the Afro-Asian members against Britain and Australia and so determined South Africa's departure from the Commonwealth and its beginning as a true multiracial partnership. Canada had in 1947 already persuaded Britain and Australia to accept the idea of the Commonwealth as an association that could include republics owing no allegiance to the Queen, and this was to be the pattern for new members in the future.

The Conservative foreign minister, Howard Green, made the cause of disarmament and radiation control peculiarly his own. Although Canada's efforts did not contribute directly to the atomic test-ban treaty, they did represent in concert with the policies of many other nations the real if intangible pressure of world opinion encouraging the two great powers to arrive at their agreement. The years of Conservative power from 1957 to 1963 saw a decline in the importance of Canada's role in world affairs for which the Conservatives cannot really be held responsible. Such embarrassments as Diefenbaker's attempt to sway the Canadian ethnic vote by an inappropriate speech at the UN about captive nations under Communist rule were perhaps not as significant as they seemed at the time. A change in Canada's world position was in fact inevitable and proper once the recovery of Europe was accomplished and the rise of the Asian nations had begun.

Canada became more deeply preoccupied with her relations with the U.S., and she relied more completely than ever for her defence upon American military power. This fact did not preclude an independent initiative at the UN or anywhere else – just the opposite on appropriate occasions – but it did require the exercise of continual Canadian vigilance with respect to her own interests and those of world peace, and a mature blend of forbearance, firmness and intelligence of a kind rarely demanded of, or forthcoming from, the Canadian public in the past.

For Canadians from the beginning the overwhelm-

ing presence of the United States has been, like the weather, a matter of daily conversation and constant concern. Though he spoke of Canada as "this semi-independent and irresponsible agent," President Ulysses Grant did recognize when he signed the Treaty of Washington in 1871 that the new Dominion might possibly become the permanent occupant of the northern half of the continent. But it was to be another two generations before many congressmen and editorial writers could quite manage to think of Canada as more than temporarily alienated U.S. property. Not to be outdone, the Canadian military establishment, casting about for a potential enemy after the Kaiser had been disposed of in 1918, reverted to the spirit of 1812 and devised Defence Scheme No. 1 – for use in the eventuality of armed invasion by the United States. This plan was still being circulated as a top-secret document in 1926 among the Canadian military districts, though it had already dawned on some observers that the three-thousand-mile border had been so long undefended mainly because it had become undefendable. The new realities of Canada's relations with the United States after World War I had already been expressed by Arthur Meighen's first Conservative government. And by 1940, King had committed Canada to a full alliance with the U.S. for the defence of North America. After the NORAD agreement of 1957, continental air defence was placed under joint American-Canadian command.

The Canadian and American economies had been growing more closely integrated since the beginning of the twentieth century. Canada and the United States during the 1950s were each other's best customer and chief supplier. Canada regularly bought between half and three-quarters of all her imports from the United States. She in turn supplied almost a quarter of America's imports. In 1900 over eighty percent of foreign investment in Canada was British. By 1950 eighty percent was American. Well over half Canada's resource and manufacturing industries were owned in the U.S. Many of the big industrial trade unions which became established in Canada during the 1940s were Canadian affiliates of counterparts in the United States. Though they were run by Canadian officers, subject to Canadian law, and usually members of the Canadian Labour Congress, these international unions, like the American-owned industries, did pose delicate problems of jurisdiction. They could be a threat to Canada's sovereignty if Canadians and their elected representatives were willing to let them be. Whether they were willing or not, of course, every bit of Canadian sovereignty in all these fields was subject to severe limits. In the complexities of the mid-twentieth century, indeed, no government or public body (not even American ones) could escape the pressures of competing claims to power and the necessity of interdependence.

The continued intermingling of the Canadian and American peoples and their cultures has been for Canadians a cause for mounting concern. Canadians in the twentieth century read more American magazines and books than they did their own, and since 1950 have watched more American television. In 1950 there were more former Canadians in the United States than there were natives of any other foreign country except Italy, over one million in all, and several times that number born of a Canadian parent. People in the professions were particularly inclined to emigrate to the United States. The callings of about thirty percent of the Canadians who moved to the United States in 1961, for example, were listed as professional or managerial in character. But as long as four times as many dollars per capita were spent in the United States as in Canada on scientific research and development, as long as the percentage of professional workers in the American labour force was twice that of the Canadian, as long as Americans were willing to pay for universities of the calibre of M.I.T. and Stanford and Michigan while Canadians were not (although for other than monetary reasons one such Canadian institution, Toronto, might possibly be included among the two dozen great universities of North America), the attraction of the United States for highly trained Canadians would undoubtedly continue.

In spite of the fact that there were still almost five times as many Canadians moving south as Americans moving north in the 1960s, migration had been a two-way street throughout Canadian history. Among the American citizens who have become Canadians are William Van Horne and C. D. Howe – without whose labours Canada's destiny might well have taken a different course. American export of capital and technical information, as well as men, has been a major influence in helping Canada attain the world's second highest living standard. So, too, the very proximity and example of the United States have been more stimulating than inhibiting. More than that, the American presence has been one of the means, when Canadians have chosen to use it, of paying for their desire to remain independent, and cultivating those deep national differences from the United States that our history and geography have given us.

This is the cultural embrace: Canadians read more American books and magazines than Canadian ones.

vating those deep national differences from the United States that our history and geography have given us. The fact that Andrew Carnegie paid for so many of Canada's first public libraries, and that American foundations financed most Canadian research in the humanities and social sciences until Canadian organizations were ready to take over that role in the late 1950s, has not diminished or threatened Canadian identity, but rather fostered it. York University in 1965, like many others in Canada, was not really the less Canadian because half its staff had received some of their graduate training in the United States, and a third of that number were actually American citizens.

Canada has always needed not less but far more exposure to the best in American culture. It is not merely that Melville and Thoreau and Mark Twain, Frank Lloyd Wright and T. S. Eliot and Jackson Pollock

This is the American presence: John F. Kennedy (and Jackie) with Gov.-Gen. Vanier in 1961.

are part of the heritage of every man in the modern world. They are peculiarly relevant to the Canadian experience, in a way that their British and French counterparts are not; they can tell Canadians a great deal about themselves.

Nevertheless, living next door to the most powerful and dynamic nation on earth has not been easy for Canadians. It has been responsible for the central neurosis of Canadian history; and the fact that Americans in the second half of Canada's first century were friendly and generous and well disposed rather than the opposite has in some ways made the problem more difficult. Quite understandably, most informed Americans have been profoundly ignorant of the true nature of Canadian society. For months on end the only thing Canadian about most American newspapers, except for the occasional mention of an arctic coldfront, was the pulp it was printed on. Since 1963, it is true, there has been a wave of thoughtful and penetrating articles on Canadian subjects in American magazines. These may well have been partly the result of such rude manifestations of Canadian nationalism as Diefenbaker's little vendetta with President Kennedy, which had its climax in the recall of the Canadian ambassador from Washington, and later perhaps the brief spell of bomb-throwing by a little terrorist group among French-Canadian separatists. Certainly on the public, as opposed to the diplomatic, level such things seem to have had an effect on American awareness of Canada that more polite noises in the past have not had. Did many Americans care about or even notice the *Globe and Mail*'s editorials of protest against American policy during the Suez Crisis, placed as paid advertisements in the New York *Times* in 1956? What Americans were aware that the suicide in 1957

of one of Canada's great public servants, Herbert Norman, was the result of persistent and vicious use of his name and record by an American Senate committee and its counsel? When they discovered that Canadians were willing to trade on a massive scale with Communist China and even wished to recognize the existence of that country, or when they realized that Canada persisted in being civil to Castro's Cubans, Americans were often puzzled and annoyed. But these deviations of Canadian foreign policy were merely symptoms of certain differences between the two North American societies which though not obvious are nonetheless profound.

It is not due to any abnormal amount of Canadian luck or virtue that the phenomenon of a McCarthy, or a Goldwater, with his massive popular support and his even larger company of fearful or half convinced fellow travellers, simply could not have happened in Canada. Those phenomena stem from the strengths as well as the weaknesses of an ideology and a tradition that is completely alien to Canadian history. James Eayrs has observed that President Lyndon Johnson, "with the best intentions in the world, when he made his first official reference to the difficulties of the Canadian-American relationship, said that they are 'kind of like problems in the home town.' They are kind of not like that at all. They are not the problems of neighbours living together in one big home town, but of friendly foreign powers." What is surely required to avoid both the proverbial well-informed malevolence of Canadians about the United States, and benevolent ignorance of Americans about Canada, is a recognition on both sides of the foreignness and the differences, as well as the friendliness and the similarities, that lie between their two societies.

THE GREAT
FRONTIER BOOM

On the razor's edge of a mile-high mountain peak in the Cassiar country of northern British Columbia lies a sultan's ransom in asbestos ore. Since 1954, men have been clawing it out of the rock at the rate of half a million tons a year. This mine in the clouds is only one of many postwar finds that changed the economy of Canada and underwrote the postwar rise in our scale of living. Across the land, from Keno Hill to Burnt Creek, from Leduc to Bathurst, similar treasures have been unearthed. Most of these spots have been visited by George Hunter, Canada's famous flying photographer. Four of his pictures appear on the next pages.

Liquid gold at Pincher Creek

Beneath these golden Alberta wheatfields lies a limestone ridge that carries more natural gas, light oil and sulphur than any other reserve so far known in Canada. B-A Oil's sulphur plant could easily breed new industries by providing raw materials to make such diverse products as fertilizer and synthetic rubber.

Unlimited power at Kitimat

The most famous boom town in Canada, eventually planned for a population of fifty thousand, lies on a once-obscure Pacific Coast inlet. Here, hydro power generated through a mountain tunnel feeds one of the world's great aluminum smelters. As power grows expensive, such plants must move farther into the north.

Giant new docks at Sept Isles

Canada's newest seaport is Sept Isles Bay on the St. Lawrence, where ore from the iron country of Labrador pours in by rail. This is Pointe Noire, Wabush Mines' three-hundred-million-dollar terminal across the bay from the Iron Ore Company's docks. It's fed by the largest continuous iron deposit in North America.

A fortune in rust at Steep Rock

To make this newest iron mine – the Atikokan at Steep Rock Lake, Ontario – one hundred and sixty million yards of silt had to be removed from the lake bottom. Tributary lakes were drained, stream courses changed, surface drainage dammed and this open pit dug. Three million tons of ore are scooped out of here annually.

9 OPENING THE SECOND FRONTIER

What happened to a small community of learning in Hamilton, Ontario, will serve as the epitome of Canada's radical transformation in the middle years of the twentieth century. In 1945, McMaster University was still the quiet little liberal arts college and seminary that a Liberal senator had founded, in the nineteenth century, with profits from his drygoods business. It was run by the Baptist Church, and its staff members were required to be of "an Evangelical Protestant" persuasion. There were a few signs of temporary disruption, like the prefabricated houses for veterans taking advantage of their DVA cheques to go back to study. Dancing on the campus had just been allowed for the first time, and such intimations of modernity as the long skirts of the New Look were to be seen on a few fashionable female undergraduates. But there had been little change since the austerity of the depression and the war years. Most undergraduates still went to the daily chapel service, and it was still possible to know each of them by name, as it had been in Cyrus Eaton's or Harold Innis's or Sylvanus Apps's student days there.

Twenty years later the original buildings were almost lost in a university city of stone and concrete. In the centre rose the elegant polyhedron of a nuclear reactor, the first one on any university campus outside the United States. The student body, which now contained the highest proportion of post-graduate students in Canada, had increased four times over and was expected to double again. A lecturer's starting salary had risen from about fifteen hundred to seven thousand dollars, more than the president had earned in 1945. At the church's initiative, the university had become a secular institution. There were new professional faculties, including medicine, and an engineering school that had particular affinities with the giant

steel and electrical industries of Hamilton. There was an honours programme in fine art, and a university department of religion where among colleagues of a variety of religious persuasions a Jesuit taught New Testament theology.

For the first time the universities of Canada, half of them founded since the war, were receiving federal government aid. Though the Canadian provinces were far behind states like California and New York in their *per capita* expenditure on education, the rising cost of universities, along with that of the expanding school systems, made education the largest item in provincial budgets. The universities no longer lived a marginal existence. They stood at the centre of an opulent urban society whose attitudes were being studied and programmed by social scientists and computers, and whose way of life was being altered beyond recognition by automation and electronics and a new industrial alchemy that seemed capable of turning any substance into anything else. Whether, as the new churches of a secular society, the universities ministered adequately in any way to the needs of man as a whole and living person (or should be expected to do so) was, however, open to doubt.

The postwar boom in the Canadian economy was unexpected. The depression had not ended in natural recovery (eleven percent of the labour force was still unemployed in 1939). Instead, it had been interrupted by the war. Most leaders of Canadian business expected depression to return almost as soon as peace did. Senior statesmen of industry shook their heads at the activities of E. P. Taylor as he bought up companies. One said that Taylor was building a house of cards.

Canadians remained the most heavily insured people in the world and the life insurance companies continued to invest a negligible amount of their money in common stocks. Canadian private investors did not put much intelligent risk capital into developing their country either. If they bought stocks at all they preferred either to take the gilt-edged security of solidly established corporations, or to gamble in penny mining stocks, Toronto's answer to Las Vegas. It was left to the exceptional few, or to government, or to foreign investors, particularly Americans, to supply the risk capital that the economy was crying for.

Nevertheless every force seemed to conspire for expansion. In 1946 the Canadian birth rate rose sharply; in 1955 it levelled off at about twenty-seven per thousand, almost double that of Britain and nearly the highest in the world. The new pensions and family allowances, along with people's war savings and the postwar rise in real wages, assured a wider distribution of wealth. There was more money to be spent on the backlog of demand for consumer goods and services. The baby bonuses alone amounted to as much as eight percent of the federal budget and their institution was soon followed by changes like the big expansion in the children's shoe industry and the rise in the number of practising pediatricians.

Because of consumer demand, the Canadian steel industry, far from cutting back production as it had been forced to do during the twenty years following World War I, achieved an amazing fivefold increase in the same period after World War II. By pioneering new methods in the 1950s it also undercut American competition for the first time. Among its first postwar customers were the agricultural implement makers, who by 1949 were selling over four times more equipment than they were in 1939. The tractor and the combine now finally replaced the horse teams and field hands on the farm. In 1939, one Canadian worker in

Sign of a new Canada: reactor on McMaster campus.

Sign of the postwar boom: fever in the stock markets.

99

every three was employed in agriculture. In 1949 the ratio was down to one in five and it looked as if by 1980 it would be only about one in thirteen. Yet the volume of agricultural production was rising. The bumper wheat crops of the 1950s were as much as four times larger than the great crops of the western wheat boom of the 1900s.

A renewed assault was made on the mineral riches of the Canadian north. With the opening of iron ore deposits in northern Quebec, Canada became for the first time a major ore-exporting nation. New oil discoveries not only transformed Alberta and blew up the size and ego of Edmonton overnight, but the effects were felt right across the country. The building of the trans-Canada pipelines for oil and natural gas along with the construction of the giant St. Lawrence Seaway buoyed up the expanding economy and like the other economic developments helped to ensure that the recession of 1957-60 would be temporary.

New towns sprang up in the far northern wilderness: Schefferville, Quebec, for iron mining; Thompson, Manitoba, for nickel; and Kitimat, British Columbia, for smelting aluminium. Canadians as a whole, however, in spite of their prime minister's vision, did not exactly become an arctic people. The MP for the Northwest Territories complained that most of his countrymen did not experience the north at all. "They just sit like great puddings in their living rooms while the sauce of television pours over them."

Certainly it was the urban revolution in the south that was the greatest of all. A million houses were put up during the 1950s and a wide band of new suburbs grew round the old city cores, larger than the original cities themselves. The pattern imposed by the automobile shattered old communities and brought complex new problems in urban living. To repair a little of the damage, provincial governments and several national bodies tried to encourage better town and country planning, though their efforts until well into the 1950s were mostly too little and too late. Metropolitan government was finally adopted as one effective beginning of a solution to the problems of urban sprawl around several large centres, and it came first of all where it was needed most, in Toronto.

No place was more affected by the midcentury boom than Metropolitan Toronto. It acquired the somewhat dubious distinction of being the fastest-growing big city in North America – in population, assessment, construction, retail trade, almost anything you could name. In 1965, the first section of a twelve-

CBC television began in 1952. Famous early face was Lorne Greene's. His fame kept on spreading.

lane expressway, the widest in the world, was opened. As mines and rumours of mines continued to spread across northern Ontario, the Toronto Stock Exchange sometimes outran New York's in the number of shares traded daily. One third of Canada's million and a half immigrants during the first dozen postwar years found their way to Metropolitan Toronto. And as they brought their relations and countrymen from Italy and Hungary and Portugal and Hong Kong and the West Indies to join them in the following decade, they helped transform the shops and restaurants and theatres of the city and make things grow that had not been there before.

With the opening of CBC television in 1952 and the expansion of the two English-language radio networks, with a boom in advertising agencies and the resurrection of trade publishing after the grim years of the depression and war, with a host of new professional and training and communications specialists at work in the city, Toronto became for the first time

The idiosyncracies and genius of pianist Glenn Gould are symbols of "a new climate of interest in the arts."

a cultural metropolis for English-speaking Canadians. A metropolis was a commodity they had found hitherto outside the country, in London and New York. The shining white, curving towers of the new city hall and the new international airport proclaimed a commitment to the best standards of international excellence in design, as well as a certain local determination to be henceforth "classic to ourselves," as Emerson had put it in heralding the American Renaissance a century earlier. Montreal's Place Ville Marie was a symbol of the senior metropolis of Canada maintaining its pride of place, and its prominence as capital of the new French-speaking nation within Canada, proud, mature and fully aware for the first time.

The story of the Quebec revolution forms the climax of Canadian political history to date, but it must be noted here that it was based on profound social and economic changes, accelerated after the war. It is significant too that its beginning should have been announced well over a decade in advance by one

of the master painters of the twentieth century, Paul-Emile Borduas, in his manifesto *Refus Global*, published in Montreal in 1947.

There was revolution, too, in the arts as Canada approached her hundredth birthday. For the first time, most notably in the performing arts and in painting and sculpture, the work of significant numbers of Canadian artists, not just that of a few isolated individuals, reached the highest standards of excellence. The old double standard ("yes, it's good, for *Canada*") was discarded at last. That a Canadian group should have won the Guggenheim International award for painting both in 1958 and 1960 was one small indication of the transformation that had taken place.

Most remarkable of all was the new climate of public acceptance and interest in the arts. As new centres for the performing arts sprang up across the country from Charlottetown to Calgary, it was clear that the artist was no longer the rejected outcast of the depression, or the irrelevant outsider of the war years and the early philistine phase of the economic boom. By 1965, a mayor or a business corporation courting public favour talked a little less about keeping the mill rate down and more about promoting the arts. Small towns suddenly saw themselves as Stratfords, and provincial capitals looked for cultural enterprises that would outshine Toronto's, or at least bring in the tourists. Parry Sound, with a population of six thousand, proposed to build a twelve-thousand-seat outdoor summer amphitheatre. It was as though the arts in Parry Sound were the modern equivalent of the ten railroads that Fort George had promised itself during Canada's earlier boom at the turn of the century. The department of transport, in building its new airports across the country, became one of the world's leading art patrons. In 1964 the federal government ruled that between one and three percent of the cost of all its new buildings must be spent on works of art, and a few universities and business corporations both led and followed the movement of public opinion in this same direction.

There was one serious flaw in the pattern. Canadians as they prepared to celebrate their first century obviously did not know how much their new interests and tastes would cost, or did not want to know. It was relatively easy to plan magnificent theatres and art galleries. Since education was now considered a thing worth spending serious money on, it was also often possible to pay for excellence in the training of artists – singers, for example, of the

New excellence in the performing arts is vividly demonstrated by singers—like Teresa Stratas.

calibre of Jon Vickers and Teresa Stratas and Léopold Simoneau and the dozens of Canadians now employed in the opera houses of Europe. But most Canadian artists were still hard pressed to make a year-round living. It is true that three national ballet companies, an opera company, and repertory theatres from Halifax to Vancouver all felt the blessing of public support. Thanks to recommendations of the Massey Commission in 1951, and death-duties on the estates of two multimillionaires in 1956, the Canada Council for the support of the arts came into being in 1957. While it has spent its money boldly and wisely, its annual budget for all the arts in Canada has amounted at the most to a little over one million dollars, which is less than half the sum the government of Austria spent annually on subsidies for just one great opera company between 1959 and 1963. During this same period Canada's defence department spent six times the amount of the Canada Council's total arts budget – an average of six million dollars annually – on military bands alone. The Stratford Festival's near-capacity houses proved that an audience could be found for excellence in Canada, but its first ten years showed also what Europeans have always taken for granted: that excellence in the performing arts requires subsidies and patrons.

It was possible in Canada in 1965 for thousands of lawyers and stockbrokers and tens of thousands of teachers to earn a satisfactory living. But there were few painters with an income tax problem, and no composers. Not a single Canadian playwright or poet could make a living from his work, and none were openly paid to be artists, even by the universities where many of them taught. Freedom to go hungry or to work at something other than their art was still one of Canada's gifts to her best creative artists in the prosperous 1960s. But at least the chance to have their work known and enjoyed, attacked and used by their countrymen was a refreshing change for the better – and, hopefully, one that could last beyond the glamour of Expo 67 and the celebration of Canada's hundredth birthday.

THE NEW CITIES

This bird's-eye view of Toronto's flamboyant new city hall, together with the photos that follow, suggests how much the face and inner soul of Canada is changing in the postwar years. It has been said confidently that in the three decades between 1950 and 1980 there will be as much physical change as there has been in the past three centuries. The transformation is almost totally urban, part of an architectural and cultural renaissance that has made town planning respectable, turned governments and business firms into patrons of the arts and put the construction industry on top as the biggest business in the land. Arthur Lower, our social historian, once wrote that Canada's narrow, colonial streets fitted Canada's narrow, colonial minds. But in the years following the war both minds and streets have begun to broaden, and for very practical reasons: the blighted downtown areas simply had to meet the competition of the new suburbs. How they have done it is shown on the following pages.

103

Curtain wall
and cruciform

Sometimes a single structure can change the attitudes of the community it serves. This was certainly true of the B.C. Electric building in Vancouver, considered by many to be the first really modern skyscraper erected in Canada. It is designed like a Douglas Fir, with a central trunk and steel branches on which are hung the glass curtain walls that provide its outer shell and allow it to serve as an electric beacon for the entire community. Montreal's Place Ville Marie, which was erected on the ugliest empty lot in Canada (three blocks of unused CNR property), was conceived in its unique cruciform shape in order to solve a difficult problem: how to build the biggest office building in Canada and still give every executive a window. Cautious businessmen at first shunned the radical structure, but came into line after the Royal Bank chose it as a head office. Now every major city in Canada wants one like it.

Building's guides relax (left) in the forecourt of Place Ville Marie. Beneath them, a modern shopping centre serves one hundred thousand.

Modern design used as part of the subtle sell: lights in Vancouver's B.C. Electric building are never turned out. Thus the entire structure is a kind of permanent commercial message.

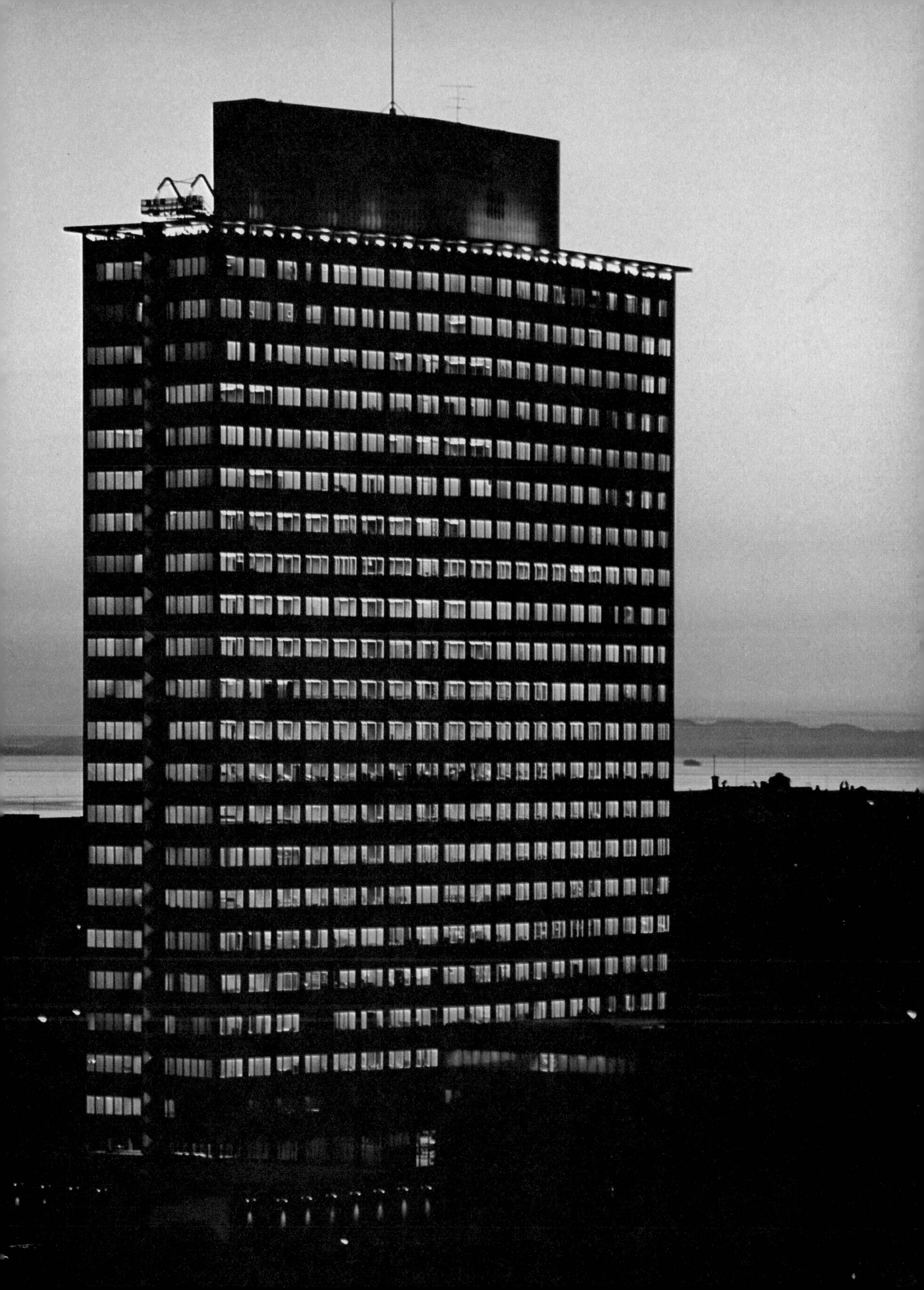

In the new airports, the government itself becomes a patron of the arts

Handsome brass screen (below), commissioned from artist Harold Town for Toronto airport, weighs one thousand pounds and required a ton of acid to etch it. The etching process took 1440 hours of hard work.

In more than a dozen modern airports across Canada, such as Toronto International (above), artists, sculptors and architects have left their imprint—often avante garde and controversial—at government expense.

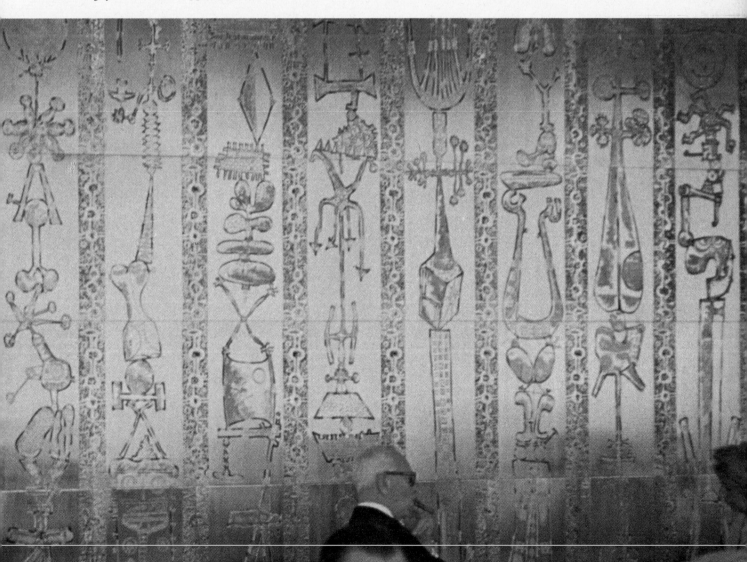

Even the politicians get behind the cultural explosion

This mad scene, unthinkable in pre-war days, took place in 1965 at the Toronto art gallery. It's a "happening" in which artist Harold Town, in dark glasses (see previous page) urged people to fling paint at a wall. The mayor was the first to oblige.

Commissioned by the province of Quebec for its new
art and trade school at Asbestos, Armand Vaillan-
court's prize-winning sculpture so enraged the citiz-
enry that three thousand petitioned for its removal.
The demand was turned down but this did not prevent
further attacks on the work, which has survived gal-
lons of paint and even sticks of dynamite. An impres-
sive offer from the Pepsi-Cola company to buy the
offending creation for seventeen thousand dollars
finally convinced most people that they had something after all. It has since become something of a
tourist attraction with visitors sending home post-
cards displaying it. The sculpture, which weighs
twenty-five thousand pounds, actually cost the artist
money. He was paid five thousand dollars in prize
money but spent twelve thousand casting it. He does
not really mind, since the publicity—two hundred
and fifty articles plus a film—was well worth it.

In north Toronto, Highway 401 is spreading to become the world's widest — at one point, 12 lanes, 15 ramps.

Planned obsolescence hits highways, too

Coiled around every major metropolis in Canada, like a strangler's loop, are the sinuous shapes of the new superhighways. Just as old cars are squeezed into scrap to be replaced by more up-to-date versions, so too do the freeways enjoy a regular model change. The interchanges, once so uncomplicated that they could be described simply as "cloverleafs," are now so unbelievably intricate that a driver who takes a wrong turn can be trapped for hours on one. And what major highway in the land can be said to be free of construction gangs, endlessly widening, repaving or straightening away, to the accompaniment of signs apologizing for the inconvenience? By the late '50s, one statistician had figured out that Canadian motorists were losing more time just getting to and from work than they were through illness. Those few pedestrians who still existed were warned by electric signs when they could and could not walk. And as our national birthday approached, more new model changes were being planned: new pedestrian walkways, two-level streets, moving sidewalks and six-lane, one-way speedways. Progress was on its way, as usual, to the accompaniment of more signs whispering, "Sorry . . ."

Old cars, squeezed into cube shapes, form an ever-increasing mountain of junk on Toronto's waterfront.

10 POLITICS FOR THE SECOND CENTURY

In the ninetieth year of Confederation it almost seemed as if Canadians had outgrown politics. The Liberal government had been in office so long that a young man not yet born when it began could now qualify to vote for it when it next sought election. As the government grew older in office, it seemed also to grow in public esteem. Rarely in modern political history had power worn a more beneficent mask. And never had the Canadian federal government been so strong, or the nation so apparently united. The finishing touches to national sovereignty – such as the abolition of appeals to the privy council in London and the appointment of the first Canadian governor-general – were being applied one by one. And Newfoundland had joined Canada to complete the pattern of Confederation conceived in 1867. The government was, in the words of one observer, not so much Liberal or Conservative as simply governmental. Its leader appeared more like a paternal sovereign than the leader of a political party. Prime Minister Louis St. Laurent's gentle upright bearing and iron grip on sanity and moderation were qualities that Canadians liked to think of as particularly their own. As no prime minister before him he embodied national unity in his own person. His very name was that of the river of Canada, and born as he was of a French-Canadian father and an Irish-Canadian mother, his childhood's first words had been uttered in Canada's two official languages. His viewpoint seemed to include that of both Canada's cultures. "Uncle Louis," like President Eisenhower, was looked up to with affection and respect and was regarded as politically unbeatable. His political managers, like those of the president, were widely supposed to have paid him the ultimate tribute of being prepared if necessary to "run him stuffed" at the next election.

The provinces of Canada repeated the pattern of mesmerized stability and quiescence. They too seemed caught in the calm of one-party rule, whether socialist in Saskatchewan or free enterprise in the two westernmost provinces; whether under the colourful and arbitrary tribal chieftains of Newfoundland and Quebec or the shrewd Conservative likeness of Uncle Louis in Ontario, who could talk through his nose as well as any farmer from the back forty. The Liberal-Progressive government of Manitoba had been in power continuously since 1922. It is true that the stronger provincial premiers had half taken over the function of opposition from the doughty but desperate little band of Conservative MPs in Ottawa. But the postwar tax rental agreements and a few easy unwritten rules about the definition of federal-provincial jurisdiction had brought something like a truce to the old political warfare between provinces and Dominion.

That was all a long time ago – in 1956. In the turbulent years that followed Canadians saw politics break out all over as it had never broken out before, in a destructive, invigorating, dynamic clash of interests. The House of Commons revived as a forum for unruly torrents of debate, flaring of tempers and extremes of passion, and even, on occasion, the conflict of ideas. In 1958 a revived Conservative Party rode to the greatest electoral victory in Canadian history. Between 1957 and 1963 three minority parliaments were elected, and for the first time since 1867 a government was decisively defeated in the House of Commons. Cabinet ministers resigned on questions of principle; the provinces erupted into new political life; and French Canada awoke from its long nightmare of subservience to Duplessis and the English-speaking financiers. The most dynamic and radical government that had ever held power in Canada took office in

Louis St. Laurent (with Vincent Massey): "As no other prime minister, he embodied national unity."

Quebec's revolution, called "quiet," was often noisy.

W. A. C. Bennett, Réal Caouette: joy for the Socreds.

Quebec in 1960. The fringes of that revolution were far from quiet or typically Canadian; terrorists planted bombs and threatened to shoot the Queen; a fat separatist Gandhi, Marcel Chaput, began a fast to the death to collect one hundred thousand dollars; Réal Caouette, a used car salesman who once admired Mussolini, with his twenty-five fellow *Créditiste* MPs, electrified the nation by seizing the balance of power in the House of Commons and in the process made French a living and much-used language there. All these forces were thrusting Canada into her second hundred years with a fury that would either see the end of Confederation or a revival in all its component parts with a vigour scarcely dreamed of by the founding fathers, or the comfortable Canadians of 1956.

The first sign of explosions to come was the pipeline debate. Through the extension of his dictatorial wartime powers C. D. Howe had been busy superintending the postwar boom – too busy to explain or defend his plans in parliament. "Who would stop us?" he asked. He and his party appeared to accept the subtly degrading old doctrine that good government is better than self-government. In April, 1956, he insisted that his scheme to help build a natural gas pipeline from Alberta east be run through parliament by an abuse of the rule of closure. And he seemed about as ready to yield to his colleagues' objections as the steel-prowed government icebreaker that had been named after him. The opposition's lively defence of the rights of parliament forced the government not merely to choke off debate but also to persuade the Speaker himself to blot out a portion of the House's business, as James Stuart had once ripped offending pages from the record of debate when he dissolved his unruly Commons in 1621. The pipeline debate became a symbol in the public mind of the arrogance of old men who had been too long in power. Critics noted that even the so-called ginger group of young Liberals in the cabinet were well into their fifties.

Many forces brought down the twenty-two-year-old government on June 10, 1957: the idleness or protest votes of Liberals who believed as religiously as people once had believed in the unsinkable *Titanic* that the Gallup polls were right about their government; sectional unrest in the west and the Maritimes after twenty years of creeping centralization; anti-American feeling; restlessness and boredom with politics as they were; a craving for leadership that could do better than remind people they never had it so good, that soothing and insulting appeal of the era of Eisenhower and Macmillan. These forces and feelings found their voice in a battling smalltown prairie lawyer who had just been elected leader of the Conservative Party. His whistle-stop, revival-meeting campaign remade the party in his own image as a party of protest – against big business, big government, the intellectual establishment and the status quo.

Of neither British nor French stock, John Diefenbaker was the first unhyphenated Canadian to be prime minister, and he brought with him into politics the sort of people who had not been there before – a Chinese MP, an Indian senator, a Ukrainian minister of labour, and, from the largest of all groups of second-class citizens, the first woman to hold cabinet rank. The city of Hamilton was plastered with MARTINI FOR DIEFENBAKER signs in 1958 – for the election of the first Italian parliamentary secretary. Diefenbaker was the first English-speaking Conservative leader to whom French Canada had given its trust since Macdonald – an astounding sixty-one percent of Quebec's popular vote in 1958.

Diefenbaker was a genuine folk hero, a battler like Harry Truman, a David assaulting Goliath, the vindicator of parliament and people, the poor newsboy who talked with Sir Wilfrid Laurier early one morning in 1910 and knew then he would be prime minister some day. He was the little man, the outsider, who had to survive nine defeats before he gained the success he always knew would be his: he failed to get elected mayor of Prince Albert; he was defeated four times in federal and provincial elections before he finally entered the House of Commons in 1940; and he was twice rejected by his party for the leadership and twice for the House leadership before the party turned to him in 1956. The strange, wild grandeur of his public manner, larger than life, was balanced by the

warmth and humour, by the feeling for local tradition and the fundamental verities, by the earnest intimacy, streaked with a talent for mockery, of his private conversation. As he said himself, his greatest sins were those of the heart; they were not cold or mortal ones, and most people for a time were as willing for him to indulge them as he was.

The difficulty was that heart-felt feelings, if they were to last, had to be translated into thought and action. Strong slogans and a nostalgia for the simpler unthinking days of Canada's rural childhood were no substitute for facing hard decisions, particularly during the difficulties of recession and unemployment which arrived at the beginning of Diefenbaker's term of office. He kept putting off decisions himself, yet would not trust his colleagues, especially the stronger ones, to make decisions of their own. He kept testing the winds of public opinion for every breeze blowing in his favour. That egocentricity and mystic relation with the common man that had made him a leader blossomed into a consuming jealousy of rivals. "Dear John" became "Ivan the Terrible." With an overwhelming majority behind him he still acted as though he were leader of the opposition. After six years in power he continued to attack "the same old bunch" and "them." But "they" were no longer just the barons of Toronto and Montreal, his own civil servants, the academic community, the Americans and the Liberal Party. "They" sometimes now included the press, the British Conservatives negotiating to enter the Common Market, possibly members of his own party, and, so it seemed at times, the city dwellers of the whole nation. The massive French-Canadian vote of confidence given him in 1958, Diefenbaker dissipated almost completely; he eventually drove his deputy leader, Léon Balcer, the most successful federal Conservative from Quebec in the twentieth century, right out of the party.

The most significant difference between Diefenbaker and his successor may well have been that Lester Pearson was a better politician. It is true that Pearson could not enjoy or dominate the proceedings of the House of Commons the way Diefenbaker did – he was apt to be petulant over trifles and too easily needled or bored. His oratory could damp the enthusiasm of the most partisan crowd. Unlike Diefenbaker, he would not be ruthless in discarding colleagues and he did not have that awesome presence or consuming self-centredness characteristic of most great political leaders. But if politics is the art of winning power by

The Chief: John Diefenbaker, here winning PC leadership in '56, was "a genuine folk hero."

Premier Jean Lesage went from reform to conservatism.

uniting your own forces, dividing the enemy, and attracting the uncommitted, then Pearson was the politician whose mastery of the art brought down Diefenbaker and won the victory for himself. In retrospect, two of Pearson's swift and lonely decisions – on nuclear weapons in January, 1963, and on the Canadian flag in April, 1964 – were the ones that ultimately split the Conservative Party and ruined his rival. They were decisions worthy of a Machiavelli or a Mackenzie King. Yet Pearson's chief motives were those of honouring commitments abroad and building a new, united Canada at home. When he could have won an easy victory that would have hurt both these causes, as in the national financial crisis that Diefenbaker managed to cover up until the day after the June election of 1962, Pearson refused to take it. As a politician he was the opposite of Machiavelli, who said it was better to be feared than to be loved. If he had a fault, it was that of trusting his colleagues too much rather than too little. He had rebuilt his party after the shattering defeat of 1958 by attracting a wide variety of uncommitted opinion. As a means of finding policies, his Kingston Conference in 1960 may possibly have been the idle ivory-tower occupation for which it was mocked by the *Globe and Mail*. But as a political symbol to attract a variety of thoughtful Canadians, and as the unintended instrument for finding workers and candidates in the next two elections, it was an unqualified success.

Pearson once admitted that if he had to live his life again he would prefer to have been UN secretary-general, seeking the *modus vivendi* out of crisis. He was not the tough, decisive leader that so many friends and critics alike cried out for him to be. Whether his role as the great compromiser and reconciler would be a success or not was still in 1965 far from being decided. But he had recognized from the outset that his major task would be to find a new status for French Canada inside Confederation, and an acceptance of that status by a consensus of the whole country.

The Quebec revolution was much more than a protest against the legacy of a charming, corrupt and autocratic leader. It was a fundamental questioning of all the institutions of French-Canadian society – it was, in one Quebec writer's words, "a revolt against ourselves, against our past deficiencies." It was "the will to become competent and to assume our rightful place in Canadian and world society." René Lévesque, the television star turned cabinet minister, proclaimed that Quebec was now "a nation awake, a nation rising, no longer content just to endure, fed up with being seen as a museum." For young French Canadians, their rebellion was particularly difficult since it had to be made not only against *duplessisme* but also, all at once, against the older generation, the Church, the Americans and English Canada. One thing many of them did not rebel against was a narrow orthodoxy of culture and opinion, and the mystic idea of race and heroic leadership of which Duplessis had been both false prophet and tin god.

In its first two years, the Lesage government was preoccupied with exposing and liquidating the worst of the Duplessis regime. English Canada applauded, unaware that it was in for a rude awakening – both *to* the true strength of French-Canadian nationalism, and *from* ignorance of its own shabby treatment of French Canada since 1867. Then, in 1963, Lesage began laying down demands; some of his colleagues and enemies did things that made him look even more conservative than he really was. English Canadians' resistance stiffened. They used words like "appeasement" for Pearson's attempt to recognize that Quebec was not a province like the others. Yet there was still no French Canadian of political stature from Quebec who also carried weight in the federal cabinet. By April, 1964, it was not easy to see how Lesage could find a stopping point, even if he wanted to, short of independent status for Quebec. Then came the agreement on the Canada Pension Plan, in the best tradition of Pearson's Suez diplomacy; the Conservatives' Fredericton Conference; and a host of other signs of a new approach from English Canada. "What is happening now in Quebec," wrote an editor of *Maclean's*, "is the struggle of a people towards those goals of political liberty and self-fulfilment which we hold most precious. It is a thrilling spectacle, and as free men we can hardly do less than cheer."

Having met a sympathetic response, several French Canadians found cause and courage to reply in kind. In September, 1964, the editor of *Le Devoir*, Claude Ryan, stated that there were two ways for French Canadians to approach their problem. One consisted of identifying French Canada with Quebec, and putting Quebec first, "by itself and for itself," as did René Lévesque and men far more radical than he. The other consisted of "the Canadian solution," not sought as a last resort but as "a reality upon which one would wish to improve." In the name of *Le Devoir*'s great founder, Henri Bourassa, Ryan declared for the Canadian solution. Those who did likewise included pragmatic

Henri Bourassa: he set out "the Canadian solution."

politicians like Lesage, business leaders like Marcel Faribault, Cardinals Roy and Léger, and above all those people who had borne the brunt of the early fighting against Duplessis – the labour unions that won their spurs in the bitter Asbestos strike of 1949, English-Canadian liberals like Frank Scott of McGill, the editors of the monthly *Cité Libre*, and a minority of intellectuals and academics, notably those who had been trained in Père G.-H. Lévesque's social science faculty at Laval. For the "Quebec solution" stood separatists of clerical, neo-fascist and socialist persuasions, the St. Jean Baptiste Society, and a majority of students, artists and intellectuals. Leaning in this direction were René Lévesque and a number of other Liberals, along with Daniel Johnson, leader of the revived *Union Nationale*.

No one could be more scathingly critical of the "escapist pursuits" of extreme Quebec nationalism than Pierre Trudeau, of *Cité Libre*. "We have expended a great deal of time and energy proclaiming the rights due our nationality, invoking our celestial mission, trumpeting our virtues, bewailing our misfortunes, and avowing our independence, and for all that not one of our workmen is the more skilled, nor a civil servant the more efficient, a financier the richer, a bishop the more learned, nor a single solitary politician the less ignorant." Yet it was clear by 1965 that thanks as much as anything to the drive of national feeling, the economic and educational aspects of the Quebec revolution would in some ways be realized. It was not yet clear in 1965 whether Quebeckers who had chosen the Canadian solution would find it viable. As *La Presse* put it, "French Canadians want to remain Canadians but on the sole condition that this does not make them second-class citizens." It was reasonable that they should wish Canada to be a place where they could feel at home anywhere. An English-speaking child could be educated in his own language, even in remote parts of Quebec like the Gaspé. But it was not possible for French children to receive French education in Regina, or even, without difficulty and sacrifice, in Toronto. English was still largely the language of business, the courts, and federal government offices outside the province of Quebec, and a French Canadian knew he could not count on using his own language in such places.

For their part, French Canadians had still to discard their smug and ignorant assumption that there was no culture in English Canada worth investigating – in spite of the fact, for example, that every major new Quebec painter of the decade before 1965 had made his reputation and sold most of his work in Toronto, Canada's art capital, before he became an important figure in his own province. By 1965 French-Canadian books and drama and television were seen frequently outside Quebec, yet the best English-Canadian writers were not commonly read by French Canadians and rarely translated. French-language newspapers did not send correspondents to Toronto or the west, though the Toronto papers had half a dozen full-time men in Quebec. French Canadians persisted in their incredible habit of describing several million countrymen of Italian, Ukrainian, Jewish, Chinese, and even Indian extraction as "Anglo-Saxons" because they happened to speak English. In an open letter to French-Canadian nationalists, Peter Gzowski, then managing editor of *Maclean's*, wrote, "We think your cause is just. You want a sense of equality in the country we inhabit in common. We agree you haven't had it, and we agree you ought to get it as quickly as possible. But we also wonder if it isn't time you listened to what we have

René Lévesque: he stands for the Quebec solution.

to say, and whether you might want to entertain some principles of ours, such as the one that nationalism isn't the most important issue in the world of 1964."

But there have been French Canadians ever since Cartier's time who have recognized the limits of nationalism and have hoped and worked for a Canada of strong but different cultures and life-styles. Laurier subscribed to Acton's view that "the co-existence of several nations under the same state is the test as well as the guarantee of freedom."

"The homeland for us," said Bourassa, "is the whole of Canada. That is, a federation of distinct races and autonomous provinces."

"Canada offers us a chance to build a new type of society," wrote Claude Ryan in 1964, "a society suited to the development of different cultures, without being rigidly or exclusively influenced by one. This idea is far from achieved in present-day Canada. But the difficulties and setbacks of the past are still not decisive enough to justify abandoning the ideal that presided at the birth of Confederation."

EPILOGUE:

THE QUEST FOR THE PEACEABLE KINGDOM

Canada is a different kind of American society, a North American alternative to the United States. Everywhere in the twentieth century man is becoming American, or to put it another way, is moving in some way towards a condition of high industrialization, affluence and leisure, instant communication, an urban man-made environment, and a mingling of cultures and traditions in a mobile, classless, global society. There is no country in the world, except the United States, which has gone farther in this direction than Canada; none that has done so in such an American way; or any that is so experienced in the art of living with, emulating and differing from the United States. If Canadians (and perhaps others) wish to explore the real freedoms open to them in such a society and to escape the blandness and boredom, the sameness and despair latent in such a brave new world, they could usefully examine the subtle but profound ways in which Canada differs from the United States.

For some purposes there are other countries with which Canada can be more profitably compared. Brazil and Australia are both, like Canada, middle-power federations whose vast lands were taken from primitive peoples and partly settled and developed by Europeans. But the contrasts are also great. The tropical jungle or desert of the southern hemisphere, the white immigration policy and British racial stock of Australia, the huge Indian population, terrible poverty and wide class differences of Brazil, set each of them apart from Canada, which in these respects is thoroughly American. Explorers of identity had best compare Canada with the United States.

When William Van Horne gave up his American citizenship after completing the CPR, he remarked, "Building that railroad would have made a Canadian out of the German Emperor." The inexorable land, like the Canadian climate, has always commanded the respect of those who have tried to master it. It is simply overwhelming. The voyager from Europe is not suddenly confronted by the rational outlines of a colossal liberty goddess; he is slowly swallowed, Jonah-like, by a twenty-two-hundred-mile-long river gulf and lake system. Coming in by air, he finds himself, scarcely past Ireland, flying above the shining blue-set islands of Bonavista-Twillingate, hours before he touches down in Toronto or Montreal. Further inland, islands come by the Thousand – or the Thirty Thousand; there are more lakes than people, and more forests than lakes. Except in small pastoral slices of southern Ontario and Quebec, the original wilderness of bush or prairie presses close to the suburban edge of every Canadian town. Even Toronto surprised a recent British visitor who called it "a million people living in a forest." In summer the boreal lights, a shaking skyful of LSD visions, can remind the most urban of Canadians that they are a northern people, that winter will bring again its hundred-degree drop in the weather, and that their wilderness stretches straight to the permafrost, the ice pack and the pole.

Nature dreadful and infinite has inhibited the growth of the higher amenities in Canada. The living has never been easy. The need to wrestle a livelihood from a cruel land has put a premium on some of the sterner virtues – frugality and caution, discipline and endurance. Geography even more than religion has made us puritans, although ours is a puritanism tempered by orgy. Outnumbered by the trees and unable to lick them, a lot of Canadians look as though they had joined them – having gone all faceless or a bit pulp-and-papery, and mournful as the evening jack-pine round the edges of the voice, as if (in Priestley's phrase) something long lost and dear were being endlessly regretted. Or there are those who run – by car, train or plane (flying more air miles per capita than any other people), lickety-split as if the spirit of the northern woods, the *Wendigo* himself, were on their trails. Nature has not always been an enemy, but she has rarely been something to be tamed either. At best we have exploited her quickly and moved on. No wonder the atmosphere of our towns still often suggests that of the mining camp or the logging drive, the trading post or the sleeping compound. If transportation has been crucial for Canada, and our main-street towns attest the worship of train and motor car, then communications (more telephone calls than anybody else), particularly radio and television (the world's longest networks), have been vital. It is no surprise when some of old Rawhide's Canadian characters become so addicted to the telegraph key that they can only talk in the dah-dah-dits of Morse code.

Survival itself is a virtue and a triumph. Images of survival abound in our popular mythologies: whooping cranes and Hutterites, dwarf ponies on the Sable Island sand dunes, the Eskimo in their howling prison of ice and snow. Ask the Nova Scotian or the French Canadian what he has done in this country of his these two or three centuries and more. "I survived," is the answer—though neither of them is satisfied with mere survival any longer.

But Canadians have also learned to live with nature and derive strength from her. It is not just the Group of Seven who came to terms with her terrible grandeur. From the first military surveyors and the CPR artists down to the abstract expressionists of post-modern Toronto, our painters have been profoundly influenced by the Canadian landscape. "Everything that is central in Canadian writing," said our great critic, Northrop Frye, "seems to be marked by the immanence of the natural world." The American critic Edmund Wilson sees the most distinguishing feature of Hugh MacLennan's work to be the unique way the author places his characters in "their geographical and even their meteorological setting." Our historians do not argue about the amount but the kind of influence geography has had on our history—whether it has been the north-south pull of North American regionalism or the east-west thrust of the St. Lawrence and Saskatchewan river systems and the Laurentian shield. The fur trade of the Pre-Cambrian forest was not only crucial to Canada's economic life for two centuries, but by 1867 it had literally determined the basic outlines of our political boundaries.

Precisely because life has been so bleak and minimal for so long in so much of Canada, the frontiers, far more than in the United States, have been dependent on the metropolitan centres of Toronto and Montreal and Europe. A visitor to pioneer Saskatchewan in 1907 remarked at the strange sight of a sod hut with a big Canadian Bank of Commerce sign on it, open for business. The essence of the Canadian west is in that image. Organized society usually arrived with the settlers or ahead of them—not only the branch bank manager, but the mounted policeman and the railway agent, the priest and the Hudson's Bay factor. Dawson City at the height of the gold rush had its sins and shortcomings, but even here lawlessness was not one of them. Violence and terror do not yet stalk the subways or the streets of darkest Toronto. The posse and the desperado belong to the American wild west, the citizen vigilante to the American metropolis.

Among peoples as different as the Métis and the Doukhobors, the community and its custom was the dominating force in western settlement. Even the most self-reliant Protestant pioneer in Canada West or Alberta was never quite a Davy Crockett or a Daniel Boone. From the founding of the Hudson's Bay Company in 1670 to that of the CPR and the dozens of modern crown corporations, the large, centrally planned enterprise, dominating its field and supported by government regulation, has been typical of Canadian development. As the historian William Morton says, Canada, in contrast to the United States, is founded on the principle of allegiance rather than social contract, on the organic growth of tradition rather than an explicit act of reason or assertion of the revolutionary will. The BNA Act sets up the objectives of peace, order and good government rather than those of life, liberty and the pursuit of happiness. The fact and principle of authority is established prior to the fact and principle of freedom. In the British tradition of monarchy, parliament and law, specific liberties are carved out within the ordered structure of society. There is in Canadian political, business and social life a certain formality and conservatism that reflect this fact. This conservatism has its regrettable side, of course. The walking dead are out in numbers— the mediocrats, the anti-hothead vote. We are "the elected squares" to one writer and "the white baboos" to another; for our inefficiencies there is no excuse. A little talent will get you a long way in an uncompetitive society, protected by tariffs and government rewards. A Canadian has been defined as somebody who does not play for keeps. Even his anti-trust laws

fail to enforce business competition as ruthlessly as the American ones.

For a Canadian, unlike a Frenchman, Britisher or American, there has not been one dominant metropolis. The English-speaking Canadian had New York and London as well as Toronto and Montreal, and for the French Canadian there has been Paris as well. This condition breeds a divided vision, sometimes paralyzing, sometimes detached and ironic, always multiple, and useful for living in the electronic age's global village. It has meant that Canadians have been better interpreters and critics of culture than creators of it – great performing musicians and actors, for example, but few good composers or playwrights. In politics and diplomacy this has led to an extreme pragmatism. Our two major parties are even less the preserve of one class or doctrine than the American parties. Certainly there has been nothing like the Republicans' monopoly of the rich and the free enterprise creed. There are no strong ideological overtones about the

Canadian approach to other peoples and world affairs.

When a distinguished American socialist advocate of free love and pacifism was turned back by Canadian immigration authorities in 1965, the liberal governor of Minnesota deplored this unexpected evidence of McCarthyism in Canada. It was of course nothing of the kind. In a sense, it was just the opposite – an almost touchingly stupid application of the letter of the law, born of respect for regulations. There was little real concern about doctrines. In Canada ideas abound and rebound with Hindu proliferation, and except among some French Canadians are not taken very seriously anyway.

There is a lingering aura of the European established church in Canada which is very different from the American separation of church and state and its consequence – the political religion of America that is increasingly prevalent in Washington and in the American intellectual establishment. The Canadian churches' influence and status can be a strain on some

people's liberties, but they are also a bastion against the more absolute dogma of an all-embracing spiritual patriotism. Canada is a land of no one ideology, no single vision; it is a cultural freeport, a way station for travellers (who often move on soon to the other America), a no-man's-land even or at least no abiding city, a place not easily confused with paradise or the promised land. This "indigestible Canada," this Marx Brothers' Freedonia, this Austro-Hungary of the new world, with its two official peoples and its multitudes of permitted ones, its ethnic islands and cultural archipelagos, its ghettos of the unpasteurized and un-homogenized, this harbour of old Adams unable or unwilling to be reborn or to burn just yet their old European clothes, but growing attached, many of them, as deeply as the Indian or the pioneer to the landscape of farm and city – this Canada has, alas, not even carried *this* characteristic as far as it might (per-haps lest it become a principle), since in practice it has been extremely difficult for Asians and West

Indians to immigrate to Canada. (The first use of the newly acquired Canadian navy in 1914 was to escort an unwanted shipload of Sikhs out of Vancouver harbour.) Hopefully one conjures up a vision of the year 2067 in which the majority of Canadians will be of Chinese origin – though the ones that speak English, who will be called "Anglo-Saxons" in Quebec, will undoubtedly have their quarrels with those who speak French, some of whom will be unable to get their children taught in French in British Columbia.

Canadians often apologize for or feel guilty about the lack of revolution or civil war in their history to stir up their phlegmatic souls. The poet James Reaney recalls someone at a cocktail party sneering at one of the Riel rebellions because so few people were killed. "What on earth would he be satisfied with? Tambur-laine's pyramid of human skulls?" Many new nations, from the United States to Indonesia, have found it necessary to make war almost immediately on other people in order to prove their own virility. Canadians have gone to war chiefly because other people in distant parts of the earth have been invaded. They have not even held any imperial possessions, like those of Australia and New Zealand. Just a bit more easily than Englishmen or Americans, Canadians can imagine what it was like to be an Indian in Gandhi's day, a Chinese at the time of the Boxer Rebellion, or a Dominican rebel in 1965. We have been invaded by the forces of manifest destiny four times, and we have been a nation of defeated peoples, a refuge of exiles, from the beginning. Canadian history has been a passion rather than an action. It has been, as one writer put it, "a stolid and phlegmatic struggle against heavy odds. Canadians dealt as a rule with forces beyond their control, in many cases the byproducts of other lands. 'Courage in Adversity,' the motto of the old Nor'wester, remained a stark national necessity for the Canadian brigades that shot the rapids and toiled across the portages of their stormy history."

The Canadian hero in the poetry of Ned Pratt is the anonymous representative of a beleaguered society, who has confronted and survived both the "grey shape of the palaeolithic face," and the diabolic, shrill commands of the "Great Panjandrum," Pratt's symbol for "the mechanical power of the universe, who controls the stars, the movement of matter, the automatic instincts of living things, even of reason and consciousness," that Prince of Darkness who thinks he is God. The hero's real source of strength is his knowledge that the Panjandrum is not God, "that for him there can be no God who has not also been a human being, suffered with the beleaguered society, yielded to the power of death and yet conquered it."

To identify that which is most essentially Canadian in our literature, Northrop Frye recalls a painting, The Peaceable Kingdom, which depicts a treaty between Indians and Quakers, and a group of animals, lions, bears, oxen, illustrating the prophecy of Isaiah; it is a haunting and serene vision of the reconciliation of man with man and man with nature. Frye suggests the Canadian tradition as revealed in literature might well be called a quest for the peaceable kingdom.

In a world where independence often arrives with swift violence, it may be good to have one nation where it has matured slowly; in a world of fierce national prides, to have a state about which it is hard to be solemn and religious without being ridiculous, and impossible to be dogmatic. In a world with tendencies to political division and cultural homogeneity,

Canada is a country moving in the opposite direction – towards political federation and cultural and regional variety. In a world that strives for absolute freedom and often gains only oppressive power, Canada presents a tradition that sees freedom in a subtle creative tension with authority; in a world of vast anonymous power elites, Canada is a society whose leaders number no more than Aristotle's five thousand and can know each other personally without being stifled or hopelessly parochial. In a world haunted by the fear of overpopulation, one is grateful for a place with room for more. In a world of striving for moral victories, it is good to have a country where a sort of moral disarmament is possible. ("You and your goddam moral victories," says an Arthur Miller character who might well be a Canadian. "We're killing one another with abstractions. Why can't we ever speak *below* the issues?") In a world of ideological battles, it is good to have a place where the quantity and quality of potential being in a person means more than what he believes; in a masculine world of the assertive will and the cutting edge of intellect, a certain Canadian tendency to the amorphous permissive feminine principle of openness and toleration and acceptance offers the possibility of healing.

The Fathers of Confederation chose the title "Dominion" for the country they had made. Typically it was a second choice, after their British rulers rejected the title they wanted. It comes from the Hebrew scriptures, the seventy-second psalm, a few other words from which may serve as a loose-fitting epigraph to what we have been saying here, as well as some sort of ground from which the good hope of another hundred years may spring.

"Let men flourish out of the city like grass upon the earth / Let there be an abundance of grain in the land / The mountains also shall bring peace, and the hills righteousness unto the people / He shall come down like rain upon the mown grass, even as the showers that water the earth / Let all nations call him happy, let his name continue as long as the sun / For he shall deliver the poor when he cries, the needy also and him that has no helper / Let his dominion also be from sea to sea, and from the river unto the world's end / And blessed be the name of his majesty forever. Amen and Amen."

And amen too to this brief beginning of our nation's history.

FURTHER READING AND ACKNOWLEDGMENTS

Anyone familiar with Canadian historical writing over the past few years will recognize how much this book owes to the work of a number of Canadian historians. In addition to the particular books cited in the text or in the notes below, the excellent one-volume histories of Canada by Donald Creighton, Arthur Lower, Edgar McInnis and William Morton are especially recommended for further reading. So, too, are these books: Frank Underhill, *The Image of Confederation* and *In Search of Canadian Liberalism*; William Morton, *The Canadian Identity*; James Eayrs, *Northern Approaches* (mainly on Canadian foreign relations); Harry Johnson, *The Canadian Quandary* (mainly on economic policy); a CIPA booklet, *The Price of Being Canadian*; a book of essays on French Canada by G. R. Cook to be published in 1966; and a collection of recent prose exploring the Canadian identity which I have edited for publication by Macmillan's of Canada in 1966. The best brief introduction to the study of Canadian government is John Saywell and John Ricker, *How We Are Governed*. For the study of primary source material, *Canadian Historical Documents*, Vol. III, edited by R. C. Brown and Margaret Prang, a lively set of illustrations of Canada's history (to which this book owes a particular debt) is especially recommended. There have been a number of interesting books on Canadian history by leading Canadian journalists, of which I found Ralph Allen's *Ordeal by Fire*, Peter Newman's *Renegade in Power*, and Bruce Hutchison's *Mr. Prime Minister* the most stimulating. For Canadian social history since 1867 see Part III of Arthur Lower's *Canadians in the Making*, the footnotes of which refer to many magazines and books used in the preparation of this book. *The Literary History of Canada*, edited by Carl Klinck, is the best guide to the creative writing of this period, and also contains essays on the writing of Canadian history.

The quotation from Douglas LePan in the Introduction is to be found in his essay in the *Atlantic Monthly*'s supplement on Canada, November, 1964. The other brief quotation is from Patrick Anderson's "Poem on Canada": I am one and none . . . / America's attic, an empty room, / A something possible, a chance, a dance / That is not danced. A cold kingdom. The pattern of the various lists of names was partly suggested by a passage in Dom Gregory Dix, *The Shape of the Liturgy*, pp. 744-5, by the list of politicians in the Introduction to a book of mine, *The Firebrand*, and by the varying final line in the stanzas of John Betjeman's poem "Dorset" (e.g. "Gloved the hands that hold the hymn book which this morning milked the cow, / While Tranter Reuben, T. S. Eliot, Edna Best and Edith Sitwell lie in Melstock churchyard now"). Mr. Betjeman notes that his names were "put in not out of malice or satire but merely for their euphony."

For background reading to Chapter 1, Donald Creighton, *The Road to Confederation 1864-67* and P. B. Waite, *The Life and Times of Confederation* and his selections (in paperback) from *The Confederation Debates in the Province of Canada, 1865*, are recommended. The words I have selected from the speeches of Brown and Cartier were not all spoken in the order used here, and I have not pockmarked the text with dots indicating gaps. For unbroken selections from the original text see Waite, pp. 49-52 and 58-61. The other founding father quoted is D'Arcy McGee. The remark about Macdonald is from the diary of Mercy Coles, daughter of the P.E.I. politician George Coles, quoted in Creighton, p. 185. The description of Saint John makes use of material on pp. 229-30 in Waite, *Life and Times*. The remark about Halifax is from W. H. Russell, *Canada, Its Defences, Conditions and Resources* (1865). Trollope's description of Ottawa and the Parliament buildings is on pp. 68-74 of his travel book *North America*. *Toronto Called Back* (1889) and G. M. Adam, *Toronto, Old and New* (1891) and a number of newspapers of the period were also used. The account of the Fenian invasion of Canada West in Chapter 2 is based chiefly on Scadding, *Toronto Past and Present*. Other Fenian material is mainly from newspapers quoted in Waite, *Life and Times*, Chapter 15. The phrase "savings of Irish chambermaids" is from Morton, *Kingdom of Canada*, p. 341. Other books that should be consulted on Canada 1867-87 and which provide the best background to the remainder of Chapter 2 are George Stanley, *Louis Riel*, Margaret Ormsby, *British Columbia*, and Donald Creighton, *The Old Chieftain*. For Chapters 3 and 4 the files of *The Busyman's Magazine* and *Maclean's* from 1905 onwards were used extensively. The banker quoted is Edmund Walker (from his papers in the University of Toronto library). The British visitor quoted is the economist J. A. Hobson who wrote *Canada Today* (1906). The Liberal statesman quoted on the war is Newton Rowell (see Brown and Prang, *Documents*). D. C. Masters, *The Winnipeg General Strike*, and William Morton, *Manitoba*, afforded material for the first part of Chapter 5. The remark about the United Church is quoted in H. H. Walsh, *The Christian Church in Canada*, p. 299. The "700 Authors" poster is quoted in *Literary History*, p. 492. Several sentences in Chapters 6 and 7 are from my book, *The Elements Combined*. The remark about Holt is from Peter Newman, *Flame of Power*, p. 44. A participant's account of the 1935 march is in Brown and Prang, *Documents*. On Aberhart see John Irving, *Social Credit in Alberta*, and H. J. Schultz's article in the *Canadian Historical Review*, Sept., 1964. On King see the biography by R. M. Dawson and H. B. Neatby, and on Meighen, Roger Graham's biography. The quotation from Joseph Schull is in Chapter 7 of *The Far Distant Ships*, p. 124-5, and from Underhill (about King) in *Liberalism*, pp. 127-35. For colourful use of Canadian magazine and newspaper material see R. Allen, *Ordeal by Fire*. Chapter 8 is mainly based on the CIIA series of books, *Canada and World Affairs*; on the writing of Edgar McInnis; on James Eayrs's books, *In Defense of Canada* and *The Commonwealth and Suez*; and on J. S. Dickey, ed., *The U.S. and Canada* (see articles by Eayrs, John Holmes and Douglas LePan). For background to Chapter 10, see *The Canadian Annual Review* (1960-); F. Scott and M. Oliver, *Quebec States Her Case*; Hugh MacLennan, "Two Solitudes Revisited," *Maclean's*, Dec. 14, 1964; G. R. Cook's articles on French Canada in *The International Journal*, Winter, 1964-65, and in A. Rotstein, ed., *The Prospect of Change*. J.-L. Pépin's words are from *Canadian Forum*, Dec., 1964; Claude Ryan's from a translation in *The Globe and Mail*, Sept. 22, 1964; Peter Gzowski's from *Maclean's*, Oct. 22, 1964; and the *La Presse* editorial is quoted by George Bain in the *Globe and Mail*. The *Maclean's* editor quoted is Robert Fulford (Dec. 2, 1963). The quotation from R. Lévesque is in G. R. Cook's second article cited above, and that of Pierre Trudeau in *Quebec States Her Case*, p. 61. Trudeau quotes (p. 67) the words of Acton used here. See also Mason Wade, *The French-Canadian Outlook*.

The quotations from Northrop Frye in the Epilogue are from the *Literary History*, pp. 848-50, and his introduction to E. J. Pratt, *Collected Poems* (2nd edition). The quotation from Chester Martin is in his *Foundations of Canadian Nationhood*, p. 514. The Miller play is *After the Fall*. Some of the other ideas and words in the Epilogue derive from my background notes supplied to the Duke of Edinburgh's Conference, 1962, and from the writing or conversation of Neil Compton, William Morton, Merrill Denison, Peter Newman, John Conway, Mordecai Richler, Hugh MacLennan, James Eayrs, Reeves Haggan, Msgr. A. Parent, C. D. Howe, Joyce Wieland, Stefan Stykolt and Kenneth, Mary, and Elizabeth Kilbourn. The arrangement of the seventy-second Psalm is made up from the translation in the Book of Common Prayer.

INDEX

PICTURE CREDITS

Order of appearance in the text of pictures listed here is left to right, top to bottom. After the first recording, principal sources are credited under these abbreviations: Alberta Government Photograph, from the Ernest Brown Collection, EB; Canadian Pacific, CP – Canada Wide Photo, CW – Ralph Greenhill Collection, RGC – Glenbow Foundation Photograph, GF – Manitoba Archives, MA – National Aviation Museum, Ottawa, NAM – National Film Board, NFB – The National Gallery of Canada, Ottawa, NG – Ontario Archives, OA – The Public Archives of Canada, PA.

Cover: The Public Archives of Canada; 2: National Aviation Museum, Ottawa – 4: Ralph Greenhill Collection (from Miller Services) – 8: PA – 11: PA – 13: PA – 14: PA – 15: PA – 16: PA – 17: Ontario Archives; PA – 18: PA; PA; PA – 19: PA; PA; RGC – 23: RGC – 24: PA – 25: Phil Shackleton (from Miller Services) – 27: OA – 28: PA; PA – 29: PA; OA – 30: Alberta Government Photograph, from the Ernest Brown Collection; PA – 31: OA; PA – 32: EB; PA; PA – 33: PA – 35: PA – 36: Glenbow Foundation Photograph; GF; GF – 37: PA – 38: PA – 39: PA; PA – 40: PA; PA; John Miller, from Page Toles – 41: PA; PA; PA – 42: John Miller; PA; Canadian Pacific – 43: EB; CP – 44: EB; EB; PA – 45: PA – 46: PA – 49: PA – 50: Baker Advertising Agency Limited; PA – 51: PA – 52: The National Gallery of Canada, Ottawa – 53: NG – 54: NG – 55: NG – 56: NG; NG – 57: NG; NG – 59: Manitoba Archives; MA, from the Foote Collection – 61: NAM; GF – 62: NAM; NAM; NAM; GF; NAM – 63: NAM; NAM; NAM; NAM; NAM – 64: NAM; NAM; NAM; NAM; NAM – 65: NAM; NAM – 67: Alexandra Studio; Fednews – 68: Toronto Star Syndicate; Alexandra Studio – 69: The William Kensit Studio – 70: MA – 71: PA; PA – 72: PA; PA – 73: PA; PA; PA – 74: PA – 75: Aime Dupont, New York; PA; Harris & Ewing; PA – 76: PA: PA – 77: PA; PA – 79: National Film Board – 80: The Telegram, Toronto; PA – 81: NFB – 82: PA; The Moon, Toronto; Moon – 83: PA; PA; Moon – 86: Horst Ehricht – 89: NFB; National Defense Photograph – 91: Henri Rossier (from Miller Services) – 92: Don Newlands – 93: George Hunter – 94: George Hunter – 95: George Hunter – 96: George Hunter – 97: George Hunter – 99: Tom Bochsler; Toronto Star – 100: CBC Still Photo Department – 101: Paul Rockett – 102: Don Newlands – 103: Don Newlands – 104: Canada Wide Photo – 105: George Hunter – 106: George Hunter; John de Visser – 108: Michel Lambeth – 109: CW – 110: John de Visser – 111: Toronto Star Weekly; Harold Barkley – 113: NFB; CW; CW – 115: NFB; CW – 116: PA – 117: Don Newlands – 118: Bert Bell – Design Group Advertising Artists Limited – 122: John de Visser.

➤➤➤-➤➤➤-➤➤➤-➤➤➤-➤➤➤-➤➤➤-➤➤➤-➤➤➤-➤➤➤-➤➤➤-➤➤➤--◄◄◄-◄◄◄-◄◄◄-◄◄◄-◄◄◄-◄◄◄-◄◄◄-◄◄◄-◄◄◄-◄◄◄-◄◄◄

WILLIAM KILBOURN

The author of this book is chairman of the humanities division of York University, Toronto, and was himself educated at Toronto, Oxford and Harvard universities. He has often been described as the liveliest writer among Canada's leading historians, for books like *The Firebrand*, his biography of William Lyon Mackenzie

➤➤➤-➤➤➤-➤➤➤-➤➤➤-➤➤➤-➤➤➤-➤➤➤-➤➤➤-➤➤➤-➤➤➤-➤➤➤--◄◄◄-◄◄◄-◄◄◄-◄◄◄-◄◄◄-◄◄◄-◄◄◄-◄◄◄-◄◄◄-◄◄◄-◄◄◄

Type for the text of this book is 10 point Pilgrim,
composed by T. H. Best Printing Company Limited.
It was printed in Canada on Webcoat paper
by London Printing and Lithographing Company Limited.
The case was printed by Sampson Matthews Limited,
made by W. J. Gage Limited, and bound by T. H. Best Limited.